1

THE GERMANY AND THE AGRICOLA OF TACITUS.

THE OXFORD TRANSLATION REVISED, WITH NOTES.

WITH AN INTRODUCTION BY EDWARD BROOKS, JR.

INTRODUCTION.

Very little is known concerning the life of Tacitus, the historian, except that which he tells us in his own writings and those incidents which are related of him by his contemporary, Pliny.

His full name was Caius Cornelius Tacitus. The date of his birth can only be arrived at by conjecture, and then only approximately. The younger Pliny speaks of him as *prope modum aequales*, about the same age. Pliny was born in 61. Tacitus, however, occupied the office of quaestor under Vespasian in 78 A.D., at which time he must, therefore, have been at least twenty-five years of age. This would fix the date of his birth not later than 53 A.D. It is probable, therefore, that Tacitus was Pliny's senior by several years.

His parentage is also a matter of pure conjecture. The name Cornelius was a common one among the Romans, so that from it we can draw no inference. The fact that at an early age he occupied a prominent public office indicates that he was born of good family, and it is not impossible that his father was a certain Cornelius Tacitus, a Roman knight, who was procurator in Belgic Gaul, and whom the elder Pliny speaks of in his "Natural History."

Of the early life of Tacitus and the training which he underwent preparatory to those literary efforts which afterwards rendered him a conspicuous figure among Roman literateurs we know absolutely nothing.

Of the events of his life which transpired after he attained man's estate we know but little beyond that which he himself has recorded in his writings. He occupied a position of some eminence as a pleader at the Roman bar, and in 77 A.D. married the daughter of Julius Agricola, a humane and honorable citizen, who was at that time consul and was subsequently appointed governor of Britain. It is quite possible that this very advantageous alliance hastened his promotion to the office of quaestor under Vespasian.

Under Domitian, in 88, Tacitus was appointed one of fifteen commissioners to preside at the celebration of the secular games. In the same year he held the office of praetor, and was a member of one of the most select of the old priestly colleges, in which a pre-requisite of membership was that a man should be born of a good family.

The following year he appears to have left Rome, and it is possible that he visited Germany and there obtained his knowledge and information respecting the manners and customs of its people which he makes the subject of his work known as the "Germany."

He did not return to Rome until 93, after an absence of four years, during which time his father-in-law died.

Some time between the years 93 and 97 he was elected to the senate, and during this time witnessed the judicial murders of many of Rome's best citizens which were perpetrated under the reign of Nero. Being himself a senator, he felt that he was not entirely guiltless of the crimes which were committed, and in his "Agricola" we find him giving expression to this feeling in the following words: "Our own hands dragged Helvidius to prison; ourselves were tortured with the spectacle of Mauricus and Rusticus, and sprinkled with the innocent blood of Senecio."

In 97 he was elected to the consulship as successor to Virginius Rufus, who died during his term of office and at whose funeral Tacitus delivered an oration in such a manner to cause Pliny to say, "The good fortune of Virginius was crowned by having the most eloquent of panegyrists."

In 99 Tacitus was appointed by the senate, together with Pliny, to conduct the prosecution against a great political offender, Marius Priscus, who, as proconsul of Africa, had corruptly mismanaged the affairs of his province. We have his associate's testimony that Tacitus made a most eloquent and dignified reply to the arguments which were urged on the part of the defence. The prosecution was successful, and both Pliny and Tacitus were awarded a vote of thanks by the senate for their eminent and effectual efforts in the management of the case.

The exact date of Tacitus's death is not known, but in his "Annals" he seems to hint at the successful extension of the Emperor Trajan's eastern campaigns during the years 115 to 117, so that it is probable that he lived until the year 117.

Tacitus had a widespread reputation during his lifetime. On one occasion it is related of him that as he sat in the circus at the celebration of some games, a Roman knight asked him whether he was from Italy or the provinces. Tacitus answered, "You know me from your reading," to which the knight quickly replied, "Are you then Tacitus or Pliny?"

It is also worthy of notice that the Emperor Marcus Claudius Tacitus, who reigned during the third century, claimed to be descended from the historian, and directed that ten copies of his works should be published every year and placed in the public libraries.

The list of the extant works of Tacitus is as follows: the "Germany;" the "Life of Agricola;" the "Dialogue on Orators;" the "Histories," and the "Annals."

The following pages contain translations of the first two of these works. The "Germany," the full title of which is "Concerning the situation, manners and inhabitants of Germany," contains little of value from a historical standpoint. It describes with vividness the fierce and independent spirit of the German nations, with many suggestions as to the dangers in which the empire stood of these people. The "Agricola" is a biographical sketch of the writer's father-in-law, who, as has been said, was a distinguished man and governor of Britain. It is one of the author's earliest works and was probably written shortly after the death of Domitian, in 96.

This work, short as it is, has always been considered an admirable specimen of biography on account of its grace and dignity of expression. Whatever else it may be, it is a graceful and affectionate tribute to an upright and excellent man.

The "Dialogue on Orators" treats of the decay of eloquence under the empire. It is in the form of a dialogue, and represents two eminent members of the Roman bar discussing the change for the worse that had taken place in the early education of the Roman youth.

The "Histories" relate the events which transpired in Rome, beginning with the ascession of Galba, in 68, and ending with the reign of Domitian, in 97. Only four books and a fragment of a fifth have been preserved to us. These books contain an account of the brief reigns of Galba, Otho and Vitellius. The portion of the fifth book which has been preserved contains an interesting, though rather biased, account of the character, customs and religion of the Jewish nation viewed from the standpoint of a cultivated citizen of Rome.

The "Annals" contain the history of the empire from the death of Augustus, in 14, to the death of Nero, in 68, and originally consisted of sixteen books. Of these, only nine have come down to us in a state of entire preservation, and of the other seven we have but fragments of three. Out of a period of fifty-four years we have the history of about forty.

The style of Tacitus is, perhaps, noted principally for its conciseness. Tacitean brevity is proverbial, and many of his sentences are so brief, and leave so much for the student to read between the lines, that in order to be understood and appreciated the author must be read over and over again, lest the reader miss the point of some of his most excellent thoughts. Such an author presents grave, if not insuperable, difficulties to the translator, but notwithstanding this fact, the following pages cannot but impress the reader with the genius of Tacitus.

A TREATISE ON THE SITUATION, MANNERS AND INHABITANTS OF GERMANY. [1]

1. Germany [2] is separated from Gaul, Rhaetia, [3] and Pannonia, [4] by the rivers Rhine and Danube; from Sarmatia and Dacia, by mountains [5] and mutual dread. The rest is surrounded by an ocean, embracing broad promontories [6] and vast insular tracts, [7] in which our military expeditions have lately discovered various nations and kingdoms. The Rhine, issuing from the inaccessible and precipitous summit of the Rhaetic Alps, [8] bends gently to the west, and falls into the Northern Ocean. The Danube, poured from the easy and gently raised ridge of Mount Abnoba, [9] visits several nations in its course, till at length it bursts out [10] by six channels [11] into the Pontic sea; a seventh is lost in marshes.

2. The people of Germany appear to me indigenous, [12] and free from intermixture with foreigners, either as settlers or casual visitants. For the emigrants of former ages performed their expeditions not by land, but by water; [13] and that immense, and, if I may so call it, hostile ocean, is rarely navigated by ships from our world. [14] Then, besides the danger of a boisterous and unknown sea, who would relinquish Asia, Africa, or Italy, for Germany, a land rude in its surface, rigorous in its climate, cheerless to every beholder and cultivator, except a native? In their ancient songs, [15] which are their only records or annals, they celebrate the god Tuisto, [16] sprung from the earth, and his son Mannus, as the fathers and founders of their race. To Mannus they ascribe three sons, from whose names [17] the people bordering on the ocean are called Ingaevones; those inhabiting the central parts, Herminones; the rest, Istaevones. Some, [18] however, assuming the licence of antiquity, affirm that there were more descendants of the god, from whom more appellations were derived; as those of the Marsi, [19] Gambrivii, [20] Suevi, [21] and Vandali; [22] and that these are the genuine and original names. [23] That of Germany, on the other hand, they assert to be a modern addition; [24] for that the people who first crossed the Rhine, and expelled the Gauls, and are now called Tungri, were then named Germans; which appellation of a particular tribe, not of a whole people, gradually prevailed; so that the title of Germans, first assumed by the victors in order to excite terror, was afterwards adopted by the nation in general. [25] They have likewise the tradition of a Hercules [26] of their country, whose praises they sing before those of all other heroes as they advance to battle.

3. A peculiar kind of verses is also current among them, by the recital of which, termed "barding," [27] they stimulate their courage; while the sound itself serves as an augury of the event of the impending combat. For, according to the nature of the cry proceeding from the line, terror is inspired or felt: nor does it seem so much an articulate song, as the wild chorus of valor. A harsh, piercing note, and a broken roar, are the favorite tones; which they render more full and sonorous by applying their mouths to their shields. [28] Some conjecture that Ulysses, in the course of his long and fabulous wanderings, was driven into this ocean, and landed in Germany; and that Asciburgium, [29] a place situated on the Rhine, and at this day inhabited, was founded by him, and named *Askipurgion*. They pretend that an altar was formerly discovered here, consecrated to Ulysses, with the name of his father Laertes

subjoined; and that certain monuments and tombs, inscribed with Greek characters, [30] are still extant upon the confines of Germany and Rhaetia. These allegations I shall neither attempt to confirm nor to refute: let every one believe concerning them as he is disposed.

4. I concur in opinion with those who deem the Germans never to have intermarried with other nations; but to be a race, pure, unmixed, and stamped with a distinct character. Hence a family likeness pervades the whole, though their numbers are so great: eyes stern and blue; ruddy hair; large bodies, [31] powerful in sudden exertions, but impatient of toil and labor, least of all capable of sustaining thirst and heat. Cold and hunger they are accustomed by their climate and soil to endure.

5. The land, though varied to a considerable extent in its aspect, is yet universally shagged with forests, or deformed by marshes: moister on the side of Gaul, more bleak on the side of Norieum and Pannonia. [32] It is productive of grain, but unkindly to fruit-trees. [33] It abounds in flocks and herds, but in general of a small breed. Even the beeve kind are destitute of their usual stateliness and dignity of head: [34] they are, however, numerous, and form the most esteemed, and, indeed, the only species of wealth. Silver and gold the gods, I know not whether in their favor or anger, have denied to this country. [35] Not that I would assert that no veins of these metals are generated in Germany; for who has made the search? The possession of them is not coveted by these people as it is by us. Vessels of silver are indeed to be seen among them, which have been presented to their ambassadors and chiefs; but they are held in no higher estimation than earthenware. The borderers, however, set a value on gold and silver for the purpose of commerce, and have learned to distinguish several kinds of our coin, some of which they prefer to others: the remoter inhabitants continue the more simple and ancient usage of bartering commodities. The money preferred by the Germans is the old and well-known species, such as the *Serrati* and *Bigati*. [36] They are also better pleased with silver than gold; [37] not on account of any fondness for that metal, but because the smaller money is more convenient in their common and petty merchandise.

6. Even iron is not plentiful [38] among them; as may be inferred from the nature of their weapons. Swords or broad lances are seldom used; but they generally carry a spear, (called in their language *framea*, [39]) which has an iron blade, short and narrow, but so sharp and manageable, that, as occasion requires, they employ it either in close or distant fighting. [40] This spear and a shield are all the armor of the cavalry. The foot have, besides, missile weapons, several to each man, which they hurl to an immense distance. [41] They are either naked, [42] or lightly covered with a small mantle; and have no pride in equipage: their shields only are ornamented with the choicest colors. [43] Few are provided with a coat of mail; [44] and scarcely here and there one with a casque or helmet. [45] Their horses are neither remarkable for beauty nor swiftness, nor are they taught the various evolutions practised with us. The cavalry either bear down straight forwards, or wheel once to the right, in so compact a body that none is left behind the rest. Their principal strength, on the whole, consists in their infantry: hence in an engagement these are intermixed with the cavalry; [46] so Well accordant with the nature of equestrian combats is the

agility of those foot soldiers, whom they select from the whole body of their youth, and place in the front of the line. Their number, too, is determined; a hundred from each canton: [47] and they are distinguished at home by a name expressive of this circumstance; so that what at first was only an appellation of number, becomes thenceforth a title of honor. Their line of battle is disposed in wedges. [48] To give ground, provided they rally again, is considered rather as a prudent strategem, than cowardice. They carry off their slain even while the battle remains undecided. The, greatest disgrace that can befall them is to have abandoned their shields. [49] A person branded with this ignominy is not permitted to join in their religious rites, or enter their assemblies; so that many, after escaping from battle, have put an end to their infamy by the halter.

7. In the election of kings they have regard to birth; in that of generals, [50] to valor. Their kings have not an absolute or unlimited power; [51] and their generals command less through the force of authority, than of example. If they are daring, adventurous, and conspicuous in action, they procure obedience from the admiration they inspire. None, however, but the priests [52] are permitted to judge offenders, to inflict bonds or stripes; so that chastisement appears not as an act of military discipline, but as the instigation of the god whom they suppose present with warriors. They also carry with them to battle certain images and standards taken from the sacred groves. [53] It is a principal incentive to their courage, that their squadrons and battalions are not formed by men fortuitously collected, but by the assemblage of families and clans. Their pledges also are near at hand; they have within hearing the yells of their women, and the cries of their children. These, too, are the most revered witnesses of each man's conduct, these his most liberal applauders. To their mothers and their wives they bring their wounds for relief, nor do these dread to count or to search out the gashes. The women also administer food and encouragement to those who are fighting.

8. Tradition relates, that armies beginning to give way have been rallied by the females, through the earnestness of their supplications, the interposition of their bodies, [54] and the pictures they have drawn of impending slavery, [55] a calamity which these people bear with more impatience for their women than themselves; so that those states who have been obliged to give among their hostages the daughters of noble families, are the most effectually bound to fidelity. [56] They even suppose somewhat of sanctity and prescience to be inherent in the female sex; and therefore neither despise their counsels, [57] nor disregard their responses. [58] We have beheld, in the reign of Vespasian, Veleda, [59] long reverenced by many as a deity. Aurima, moreover, and several others, [60] were formerly held in equal veneration, but not with a servile flattery, nor as though they made them goddesses. [61]

9. Of the gods, Mercury [62] is the principal object of their adoration; whom, on certain days, [63] they think it lawful to propitiate even with human victims. To Hercules and Mars [64] they offer the animals usually allotted for sacrifice. [65] Some of the Suevi also perform sacred rites to Isis. What was the cause and origin of this foreign worship, I have not been able to discover; further than that her being represented with the symbol of a galley, seems to indicate an imported religion. [66]

They conceive it unworthy the grandeur of celestial beings to confine their deities within walls, or to represent them under a human similitude: [67] woods and groves are their temples; and they affix names of divinity to that secret power, which they behold with the eye of adoration alone.

10. No people are more addicted to divination by omens and lots. The latter is performed in the following simple manner. They cut a twig [68] from a fruit-tree, and divide it into small pieces, which, distinguished by certain marks, are thrown promiscuously upon a white garment. Then, the priest of the canton, if the occasion be public; if private, the master of the family; after an invocation of the gods, with his eyes lifted up to heaven, thrice takes out each piece, and, as they come up, interprets their signification according to the marks fixed upon them. If the result prove unfavorable, there is no more consultation on the same affair that day; if propitious, a confirmation by omens is still required. In common with other nations, the Germans are acquainted with the practice of auguring from the notes and flight of birds; but it is peculiar to them to derive admonitions and presages from horses also. [69] Certain of these animals, milk-white, and untouched by earthly labor, are pastured at the public expense in the sacred woods and groves. These, yoked to a consecrated chariot, are accompanied by the priest, and king, or chief person of the community, who attentively observe their manner of neighing and snorting; and no kind of augury is more credited, not only among the populace, but among the nobles and priests. For the latter consider themselves as the ministers of the gods, and the horses, as privy to the divine will. Another kind of divination, by which they explore the event of momentous wars, is to oblige a prisoner, taken by any means whatsoever from the nation with whom they are at variance, to fight with a picked man of their own, each with his own country's arms; and, according as the victory falls, they presage success to the one or to the other party. [70]

11. On affairs of smaller moment, the chiefs consult; on those of greater importance, the whole community; yet with this circumstance, that what is referred to the decision of the people, is first maturely discussed by the chiefs. [71] They assemble, unless upon some sudden emergency, on stated days, either at the new or full moon, which they account the most auspicious season for beginning any enterprise. Nor do they, in their computation of time, reckon, like us, by the number of days, but of nights. In this way they arrange their business; in this way they fix their appointments; so that, with them, the night seems to lead the day. [72] An inconvenience produced by their liberty is, that they do not all assemble at a stated time, as if it were in obedience to a command; but two or three days are lost in the delays of convening. When they all think fit, [73] they sit down armed. [74] Silence is proclaimed by the priests, who have on this occasion a coercive power. Then the king, or chief, and such others as are conspicuous for age, birth, military renown, or eloquence, are heard; and gain attention rather from their ability to persuade, than their authority to command. If a proposal displease, the assembly reject it by an inarticulate murmur; if it prove agreeable, they clash their javelins; [75] for the most honorable expression of assent among them is the sound of arms.

12. Before this council, it is likewise allowed to exhibit accusations, and to prosecute capital offences. Punishments are varied according to the nature of the crime. Traitors and deserters are hung upon trees: [76] cowards, dastards, [77] and those guilty of unnatural practices, [78] are suffocated in mud under a hurdle. [79] This difference of punishment has in view the principle, that villainy should be exposed while it is punished, but turpitude concealed. The penalties annexed to slighter offences [80] are also proportioned to the delinquency. The convicts are fined in horses and cattle: [81] part of the mulct [82] goes to the king or state; part to the injured person, or his relations. In the same assemblies chiefs [83] are also elected, to administer justice through the cantons and districts. A hundred companions, chosen from the people, attended upon each of them, to assist them as well with their advice as their authority.

13. The Germans transact no business, public or private, without being armed: [84] but it is not customary for any person to assume arms till the state has approved his ability to use them. Then, in the midst of the assembly, either one of the chiefs, or the father, or a relation, equips the youth with a shield and javelin. [85] These are to them the manly gown; [86] this is the first honor conferred on youth: before this they are considered as part of a household; afterwards, of the state. The dignity of chieftain is bestowed even on mere lads, whose descent is eminently illustrious, or whose fathers have performed signal services to the public; they are associated, however, with those of mature strength, who have already been declared capable of service; nor do they blush to be seen in the rank of companions. [87] For the state of companionship itself has its several degrees, determined by the judgment of him whom they follow; and there is a great emulation among the companions, which shall possess the highest place in the favor of their chief; and among the chiefs, which shall excel in the number and valor of his companions. It is their dignity, their strength, to be always surrounded with a large body of select youth, an ornament in peace, a bulwark in war. And not in his own country alone, but among the neighboring states, the fame and glory of each chief consists in being distinguished for the number and bravery of his companions. Such chiefs are courted by embassies; distinguished by presents; and often by their reputation alone decide a war.

14. In the field of battle, it is disgraceful for the chief to be surpassed in valor; it is disgraceful for the companions not to equal their chief; but it is reproach and infamy during a whole succeeding life to retreat from the field surviving him. [88] To aid, to protect him; to place their own gallant actions to the account of his glory, is their first and most sacred engagement. The chiefs fight for victory; the companions for their chief. If their native country be long sunk in peace and inaction, many of the young nobles repair to some other state then engaged in war. For, besides that repose is unwelcome to their race, and toils and perils afford them a better opportunity of distinguishing themselves; they are unable, without war and violence, to maintain a large train of followers. The companion requires from the liberality of his chief, the warlike steed, the bloody and conquering spear: and in place of pay, he expects to be supplied with a table, homely indeed, but plentiful. [89] The funds for this munificence must be found in war and rapine; nor are they so easily persuaded to cultivate the earth, and await the produce of the seasons, as to challenge the foe, and

11

expose themselves to wounds; nay, they even think it base and spiritless to earn by sweat what they might purchase with blood.

15. During the intervals of war, they pass their time less in hunting than in a sluggish repose, [90] divided between sleep and the table. All the bravest of the warriors, committing the care of the house, the family affairs, and the lands, to the women, old men, and weaker part of the domestics, stupefy themselves in inaction: so wonderful is the contrast presented by nature, that the same persons love indolence, and hate tranquillity! [91] It is customary for the several states to present, by voluntary and individual contributions, [92] cattle or grain [93] to their chiefs; which are accepted as honorary gifts, while they serve as necessary supplies. [94] They are peculiarly pleased with presents from neighboring nations, offered not only by individuals, but by the community at large; such as fine horses, heavy armor, rich housings, and gold chains. We have now taught them also to accept of money. [95]

16. It is well known that none of the German nations inhabit cities; [96] or even admit of contiguous settlements. They dwell scattered and separate, as a spring, a meadow, or a grove may chance to invite them. Their villages are laid out, not like ours in rows of adjoining buildings; but every one surrounds his house with a vacant space, [97] either by way of security against fire, [97] or through ignorance of the art of building. For, indeed, they are unacquainted with the use of mortar and tiles; and for every purpose employ rude unshapen timber, fashioned with no regard to pleasing the eye. They bestow more than ordinary pains in coating certain parts of their buildings with a kind of earth, so pure and shining that it gives the appearance of painting. They also dig subterraneous caves, [99] and cover them over with a great quantity of dung. These they use as winter-retreats, and granaries; for they preserve a moderate temperature; and upon an invasion, when the open country is plundered, these recesses remain unviolated, either because the enemy is ignorant of them, or because he will not trouble himself with the search. [100]

17. The clothing common to all is a sagum [101] fastened by a clasp, or, in want of that, a thorn. With no other covering, they pass whole days on the hearth, before the fire. The more wealthy are distinguished by a vest, not flowing loose, like those of the Sarmatians and Parthians, but girt close, and exhibiting the shape of every limb. They also wear the skins of beasts, which the people near the borders are less curious in selecting or preparing than the more remote inhabitants, who cannot by commerce procure other clothing. These make choice of particular skins, which they variegate with spots, and strips of the furs of marine animals, [102] the produce of the exterior ocean, and seas to us unknown. [103] The dress of the women does not differ from that of the men; except that they more frequently wear linen, [104] which they stain with purple; [105] and do not lengthen their upper garment into sleeves, but leave exposed the whole arm, and part of the breast.

18. The matrimonial bond is, nevertheless, strict and severe among them; nor is there anything in their manners more commendable than this. [106] Almost singly among the barbarians, they content themselves with one wife; a very few of them excepted, who, not through incontinence, but because their alliance is solicited on

12

account of their rank, [107] practise polygamy. The wife does not bring a dowry to her husband, but receives one from him. [108] The parents and relations assemble, and pass their approbation on the presents—presents not adapted to please a female taste, or decorate the bride; but oxen, a caparisoned steed, a shield, spear, and sword. By virtue of these, the wife is espoused; and she in her turn makes a present of some arms to her husband. This they consider as the firmest bond of union; these, the sacred mysteries, the conjugal deities. That the woman may not think herself excused from exertions of fortitude, or exempt from the casualties of war, she is admonished by the very ceremonial of her marriage, that she comes to her husband as a partner in toils and dangers; to suffer and to dare equally with him, in peace and in war: this is indicated by the yoked oxen, the harnessed steed, the offered arms. Thus she is to live; thus to die. She receives what she is to return inviolate [109] and honored to her children; what her daughters-in-law are to receive, and again transmit to her grandchildren.

19. They live, therefore, fenced around with chastity; [110] corrupted by no seductive spectacles, [111] no convivial incitements. Men and women are alike unacquainted with clandestine correspondence. Adultery is extremely rare among so numerous a people. Its punishment is instant, and at the pleasure of the husband. He cuts off the hair [112] of the offender, strips her, and in presence of her relations expels her from his house, and pursues her with stripes through the whole village. [113] Nor is any indulgence shown to a prostitute. Neither beauty, youth, nor riches can procure her a husband: for none there looks on vice with a smile, or calls mutual seduction the way of the world. Still more exemplary is the practice of those states [114] in which none but virgins marry, and the expectations and wishes of a wife are at once brought to a period. Thus, they take one husband as one body and one life; that no thought, no desire, may extend beyond him; and he may be loved not only as their husband, but as their marriage. [115] To limit the increase of children, [116] or put to death any of the later progeny [117] is accounted infamous: and good habits have there more influence than good laws elsewhere. [118]

20. In every house the children grow up, thinly and meanly clad, [119] to that bulk of body and limb which we behold with wonder. Every mother suckles her own children, and does not deliver them into the hands of servants and nurses. No indulgence distinguishes the young master from the slave. They lie together amidst the same cattle, upon the same ground, till age [120] separates, and valor marks out, the free-born. The youths partake late of the pleasures of love, [121] and hence pass the age of puberty unexhausted: nor are the virgins hurried into marriage; the same maturity, the same full growth is required: the sexes unite equally matched [122] and robust; and the children inherit the vigor of their parents. Children are regarded with equal affection by their maternal uncles [123] as by their fathers: some even consider this as the more sacred bond of consanguinity, and prefer it in the requisition of hostages, as if it held the mind by a firmer tie, and the family by a more extensive obligation. A person's own children, however, are his heirs and successors; and no wills are made. If there be no children, the next in order of inheritance are brothers, paternal and maternal uncles. The more numerous are a man's relations and kinsmen, the more comfortable is his old age; nor is it here any advantage to be childless. [124]

21. It is an indispensable duty to adopt the enmities [125] of a father or relation, as well as their friendships: these, however, are not irreconcilable or perpetual. Even homicide is atoned [126] by a certain fine in cattle and sheep; and the whole family accepts the satisfaction, to the advantage of the public weal, since quarrels are most dangerous in a free state. No people are more addicted to social entertainments, or more liberal in the exercise of hospitality. [127] To refuse any person whatever admittance under their roof, is accounted flagitious. [128] Every one according to his ability feasts his guest: when his provisions are exhausted, he who was late the host, is now the guide and companion to another hospitable board. They enter the next house uninvited, and are received with equal cordiality. No one makes a distinction with respect to the rights of hospitality, between a stranger and an acquaintance. The departing guest is presented with whatever he may ask for; and with the same freedom a boon is desired in return. They are pleased with presents; but think no obligation incurred either when they give or receive.

22. [129] [Their manner of living with their guest is easy and affable] As soon as they arise from sleep, which they generally protract till late in the day, they bathe, usually in warm water, [130] as cold weather chiefly prevails there. After bathing they take their meal, each on a distinct seat, and a a separate table. [131] Then they proceed, armed, to business, and not less frequently to convivial parties, in which it is no disgrace to pass days and nights, without intermission, in drinking. The frequent quarrels that arise amongst them, when intoxicated, seldom terminate in abusive language, but more frequently in blood. [132] In their feasts, they generally deliberate on the reconcilement of enemies, on family alliances, on the appointment of chiefs, and finally on peace and war; conceiving that at no time the soul is more opened to sincerity, or warmed to heroism. These people, naturally void of artifice or disguise, disclose the most secret emotions of their hearts in the freedom of festivity. The minds of all being thus displayed without reserve, the subjects of their deliberation are again canvassed the next day; [133] and each time has its advantages. They consult when unable to dissemble; they determine when not liable to mistake.

23. Their drink is a liquor prepared from barley or wheat [134] brought by fermentation to a certain resemblance of wine. Those who border on the Rhine also purchase wine. Their food is simple; wild fruits, fresh venison, [135] or coagulated milk. [136] They satisfy hunger without seeking the elegances and delicacies of the table. Their thirst for liquor is not quenched with equal moderation. If their propensity to drunkenness be gratified to the extent of their wishes, intemperance proves as effectual in subduing them as the force of arms. [137]

24. They have only one kind of public spectacle, which is exhibited in every company. Young men, who make it their diversion, dance naked amidst drawn swords and presented spears. Practice has conferred skill at this exercise; and skill has given grace; but they do not exhibit for hire or gain: the only reward of this pastime, though a hazardous one, is the pleasure of the spectators. What is extraordinary, they play at dice, when sober, as a serious business: and that with such a desperate venture of gain or loss, that, when everything else is gone, they set

14

their liberties and persons on the last throw. The loser goes into voluntary servitude; and, though the youngest and strongest, patiently suffers himself to be bound and sold. [138] Such is their obstinacy in a bad practice—they themselves call it honor. The slaves thus acquired are exchanged away in commerce, that the winner may get rid of the scandal of his victory.

25. The rest of their slaves have not, like ours, particular employments in the family allotted them. Each is the master of a habitation and household of his own. The lord requires from him a certain quantity of grain, cattle, or cloth, as from a tenant; and so far only the subjection of the slave extends. [139] His domestic offices are performed by his own wife and children. It is usual to scourge a slave, or punish him with chains or hard labor. They are sometimes killed by their masters; not through severity of chastisement, but in the heat of passion, like an enemy; with this difference, that it is done with impunity. [140] Freedmen are little superior to slaves; seldom filling any important office in the family; never in the state, except in those tribes which are under regal government. [141] There, they rise above the free-born, and even the nobles: in the rest, the subordinate condition of the freedmen is a proof of freedom.

26. Lending money upon interest, and increasing it by usury, [142] is unknown amongst them: and this ignorance more effectually prevents the practice than a prohibition would do. The lands are occupied by townships, [143] in allotments proportional to the number of cultivators; and are afterwards parcelled out among the individuals of the district, in shares according to the rank and condition of each person. [144] The wide extent of plain facilitates this partition. The arable lands are annually changed, and a part left fallow; nor do they attempt to make the most of the fertility and plenty of the soil, by their own industry in planting orchards, inclosing meadows, and watering gardens. Corn is the only product required from the earth: hence their year is not divided into so many seasons as ours; for, while they know and distinguish by name Winter, Spring, and Summer, they are unacquainted equally with the appellation and bounty of Autumn. [145]

27. Their funerals are without parade. [146] The only circumstance to which they attend, is to burn the bodies of eminent persons with some particular kinds of wood. Neither vestments nor perfumes are heaped upon the pile: [147] the arms of the deceased, and sometimes his horse, [148] are given to the flames. The tomb is a mound of turf. They contemn the elaborate and costly honours of monumental structures, as mere burthens to the dead. They soon dismiss tears and lamentations; slowly, sorrow and regret. They think it the women's part to bewail their friends, the men's to remember them.

28. This is the sum of what I have been able to learn concerning the origin and manners of the Germans in general. I now proceed to mention those particulars in which they differ from each other; and likewise to relate what nations have migrated from Germany into Gaul. That great writer, the deified Julius, asserts that the Gauls were formerly the superior people; [149] whence it is probable that some Gallic colonies passed over into Germany: for how small an obstacle would a river be to

prevent any nation, as it increased in strength, from occupying or changing settlements as yet lying in common, and unappropriated by the power of monarchies! Accordingly, the tract betwixt the Hercynian forest and the rivers Rhine and Mayne was possessed by the Helvetii: [150] and that beyond, by the Boii; [151] both Gallic tribes. The name of Boiemum still remains, a memorial of the ancient settlement, though its inhabitants are now changed. [152] But whether the Aravisci [153] migrated into Pannonia from the Osi, [154] a German nation; or the Osi into Germany from the Aravisci; the language, institutions, and manners of both being still the same, is a matter of uncertainty; for, in their pristine state of equal indigence and equal liberty, the same advantages and disadvantages were common to both sides of the river. The Treveri [155] and Nervii [156] are ambitious of being thought of German origin; as if the reputation of this descent would distinguish them from the Gauls, whom they resemble in person and effeminacy. The Vangiones, Triboci, and Nemetes, [157] who inhabit the bank of the Rhine, are without doubt German tribes. Nor do the Ubii, [158] although they have been thought worthy of being made a Roman colony, and are pleased in bearing the name of Agrippinenses from their founder, blush to acknowledge their origin from Germany; from whence they formerly migrated, and for their approved fidelity were settled on the bank of the Rhine, not that they might be guarded themselves, but that they might serve as a guard against invaders.

29. Of all these people, the most famed for valor are the Batavi; whose territories comprise but a small part of the banks of the Rhine, but consist chiefly of an island within it. [159] These were formerly a tribe of the Catti, who, on account of an intestine division, removed to their present settlements, in order to become a part of the Roman empire. They still retain this honor, together with a memorial of their ancient alliance; [160] for they are neither insulted by taxes, nor oppressed by farmers of the revenue. Exempt from fiscal burthens and extraordinary contributions, and kept apart for military use alone, they are reserved, like a magazine of arms, for the purposes of war. The nation of the Mattiaci [161] is under a degree of subjection of the same kind: for the greatness of the Roman people has carried a reverence for the empire beyond the Rhine and the ancient limits. The Mattiaci, therefore, though occupying a settlement and borders [162] on the opposite side of the river, from sentiment and attachment act with us; resembling the Batavi in every respect, except that they are animated with a more vigorous spirit by the soil and air of their own country. [163] I do not reckon among the people of Germany those who occupy the Decumate lands, [164] although inhabiting between the Rhine and Danube. Some of the most fickle of the Gauls, rendered daring through indigence, seized upon this district of uncertain property. Afterwards, our boundary line being advanced, and a chain of fortified posts established, it became a skirt of the empire, and part of the Roman province. [165]

30. Beyond these dwell the Catti, [166] whose settlements, beginning from the Hercynian forest, are in a tract of country less open and marshy than those which overspread the other states of Germany; for it consists of a continued range of hills, which gradually become more scattered; and the Hercynian forest [167] both accompanies and leaves behind, its Catti. This nation is distinguished by hardier frames, [168] compactness of limb, fierceness of countenance, and superior vigor of

mind. For Germans, they have a considerable share of understanding and sagacity; they choose able persons to command, and obey them when chosen; keep their ranks; seize opportunities; restrain impetuous motions; distribute properly the business of the day; intrench themselves against the night; account fortune dubious, and valor only certain; and, what is extremely rare, and only a consequence of discipline, depend more upon the general than the army. [169] Their force consists entirely in infantry; who, besides their arms, are obliged to carry tools and provisions. Other nations appear to go to a battle; the Catti, to war. Excursions and casual encounters are rare amongst them. It is, indeed, peculiar to cavalry soon to obtain, and soon to yield, the victory. Speed borders upon timidity; slow movements are more akin to steady valor.

31. A custom followed among the other German nations only by a few individuals, of more daring spirit than the rest, is adopted by general consent among the Catti. From the time they arrive at years of maturity they let their hair and beard grow; [170] and do not divest themselves of this votive badge, the promise of valor, till they have slain an enemy. Over blood and spoils they unveil the countenance, and proclaim that they have at length paid the debt of existence, and have proved themselves worthy of their country and parents. The cowardly and effeminate continue in their squalid disguise. The bravest among them wear also an iron ring [171] (a mark of ignominy in that nation) as a kind of chain, till they have released themselves by the slaughter of a foe. Many of the Catti assume this distinction, and grow hoary under the mark, conspicuous both to foes and friends. By these, in every engagement, the attack is begun: they compose the front line, presenting a new spectacle of terror. Even in peace they do not relax the sternness of their aspect. They have no house, land, or domestic cares: they are maintained by whomsoever they visit: lavish of another's property, regardless of their own; till the debility of age renders them unequal to such a rigid course of military virtue. [172]

32. Next to the Catti, on the banks of the Rhine, where, now settled in its channel, it is become a sufficient boundary, dwell the Usipii and Tencteri. [173] The latter people, in addition to the usual military reputation, are famed for the discipline of their cavalry; nor is the infantry of the Catti in higher estimation than the horse of the Tencteri. Their ancestors established it, and are imitated by posterity. Horsemanship is the sport of their children, the point of emulation of their youth, and the exercise in which they persevere to old age. Horses are bequeathed along with the domestics, the household gods, and the rights of inheritance: they do not, however, like other things, go to the eldest son, but to the bravest and most warlike.

33. Contiguous to the Tencteri were formerly the Bructeri; [174] but report now says that the Chamavi and Angrivarii, [175] migrating into their country, have expelled and entirely extirpated them, [176] with the concurrence of the neighboring nations, induced either by hatred of their arrogance, [177] love of plunder, or the favor of the gods towards the Romans. For they even gratified us with the spectacle of a battle, in which above sixty thousand Germans were slain, not by Roman arms, but, what was still grander, by mutual hostilities, as it were for our pleasure and entertainment. [178] May the nations retain and perpetuate, if not an affection for us, at least an

animosity against each other! since, while the fate of the empire is thus urgent, [179] fortune can bestow no higher benefit upon us, than the discord of our enemies.

34. Contiguous to the Angrivarii and Chamavi backwards lie the Dulgibini, Chasauri, [180] and other nations less known. [181] In front, the Frisii [182] succeed; who are distinguished by the appellations of Greater and Lesser, from their proportional power. The settlements of both stretch along the border of the Rhine to the ocean; and include, besides, vast lakes, [183] which have been navigated by Roman fleets. We have even explored the ocean itself on that side; and fame reports that columns of Hercules [184] are still remaining on that coast; whether it be that Hercules was ever there in reality, or that whatever great and magnificent is anywhere met with is, by common consent, ascribed to his renowned name. The attempt of Drusus Germanicus [185] to make discoveries in these parts was sufficiently daring; but the ocean opposed any further inquiry into itself and Hercules. After a while no one renewed the attempt; and it was thought more pious and reverential to believe the actions of the gods, than to investigate them.

35. Hitherto we have traced the western side of Germany. It turns from thence with a vast sweep to the north: and first occurs the country of the Chauci, [186] which, though it begins immediately from Frisia, and occupies part of the seashore, yet stretches so far as to border on all the nations before mentioned, till it winds round so as to meet the territories of the Catti. This immense tract is not only possessed, but filled by the Chauci; a people the noblest of the Germans, who choose to maintain their greatness by justice rather than violence. Without ambition, without ungoverned desires, quiet and retired, they provoke no wars, they are guilty of no rapine or plunder; and it is a principal proof of their power and bravery, that the superiority they possess has not been acquired by unjust means. Yet all have arms in readiness; [187] and, if necessary, an army is soon raised: for they abound in men and horses, and maintain their military reputation even in inaction.

36. Bordering on the Chauci and Catti are the Cherusci; [188] who, for want of an enemy, long cherished a too lasting and enfeebling peace: a state more flattering than secure; since the repose enjoyed amidst ambitious and powerful neighbors is treacherous; and when an appeal is made to the sword, moderation and probity are names appropriated by the victors. Thus, the Cherusci, who formerly bore the titles of just and upright, are now charged with cowardice and folly; and the good fortune of the Catti, who subdued them, has grown into wisdom. The ruin of the Cherusci involved that of the Fosi, [189] a neighboring tribe, equal partakers of their adversity, although they had enjoyed an inferior share of their prosperity.

37. In the same quarter of Germany, adjacent to the ocean, dwell the Cimbri; [191] a small [192] state at present, but great in renown. [193] Of their past grandeur extensive vestiges still remain, in encampments and lines on either shore, [194] from the compass of which the strength and numbers of the nation may still be computed, and credit derived to the account of so prodigious an army. It was in the 640th year of Rome that the arms of the Cimbri were first heard of, under the consulate of Caecilius Metellus and Papirius Carbo; from which era to the second consulate of the

emperor Trajan [195] is a period of nearly 210 years. So long has Germany withstood the arms of Rome. During this long interval many mutual wounds have been inflicted. Not the Samnite, the Carthaginian, Spain, Gaul, or Parthia, have given more frequent alarms; for the liberty of the Germans is more vigorous than the monarchy of the Arsacidae. What has the East, which has itself lost Pacorus, and suffered an overthrow from Ventidius, [196] to boast against us, but the slaughter of Crassus? But the Germans, by the defeat or capture of Carbo, [197] Cassius, [198] Scaurus Aurelius, [199] Servilius Caepio, and Cneius Manlius, [200] deprived the Roman people of five consular armies; [201] and afterwards took from Augustus himself Varus with three legions. [202] Nor did Caius Marius [203] in Italy, the deified Julius [204] in Gaul, or Drusus, [204] Nero, [204] or Germanicus [204] in their own country, defeat then without loss. The subsequent mighty threats of Caligula terminated in ridicule. Then succeeded tranquillity; till, seizing the occasion of our discords and civil wars, they forced the winter-quarters of the legions, [205] and even aimed at the possession of Gaul; and, again expelled thence, they have in latter times been rather triumphed over [206] than vanquished.

38. We have now to speak of the Suevi; [207] who do not compose a single state, like the Catti or Tencteri, but occupy the greatest part of Germany, and are still distributed into different names and nations, although all hearing the common appellation of Suevi. It is a characteristic of this people to turn their hair sideways, and tie it beneath the poll in a knot. By this mark the Suevi are distinguished from the rest of the Germans; and the freemen of the Suevi from the slaves. [208] Among other nations, this mode, either on account of some relationship with the Suevi, or from the usual propensity to imitation, is sometimes adopted; but rarely, and only during the period of youth. The Suevi, even till they are hoary, continue to have their hair growing stiffly backwards, and often it is fastened on the very crown of the head. The chiefs dress it with still greater care: and in this respect they study ornament, though of an undebasing kind. For their design is not to make love, or inspire it; they decorate themselves in this manner as they proceed to war, in order to seem taller and more terrible; and dress for the eyes of their enemies.

39. The Semnones [209] assert themselves to be the most ancient and noble of the Suevi; and their pretensions are confirmed by religion. At a stated time, all the people of the same lineage assemble by their delegates in a wood, consecrated by the auguries of their forefathers and ancient terror, and there by the public slaughter of a human victim celebrate the horrid origin of their barbarous rites. Another kind of reverence is paid to the grove. No person enters it without being bound with a chain, as an acknowledgment of his inferior nature, and the power of the deity residing there. If he accidentally fall, it is not lawful for him to be lifted or to rise up; they roll themselves out along the ground. The whole of their superstition has this import: that from this spot the nation derives its origin; that here is the residence of the Deity, the Governor of all, and that everything else is subject and subordinate to him. These opinions receive additional authority from the power of the Semnones, who inhabit a hundred cantons, and, from the great body they compose, consider themselves as the head of the Suevi.

40. The Langobardi, [210] on the other hand, are ennobled by, the smallness of their numbers; since though surrounded by many powerful nations, they derive security, not from obsequiousness, but from their martial enterprise. The neighboring Reudigni, [211] and the Avions, [212] Angli, [213] Varini, Eudoses, Suardones, and Nuithones, [214] are defended by rivers or forests. Nothing remarkable occurs in any of these; except that they unite in the worship of Hertha, [215] or Mother Earth; and suppose her to interfere in the affairs of men, and to visit the different nations. In an island [216] of the ocean stands a sacred and unviolated grove, in which is a consecrated chariot, covered with a veil, which the priest alone is permitted to touch. He becomes conscious of the entrance of the goddess into this secret recess; and with profound veneration attends the vehicle, which is drawn by yoked cows. At this season, [217] all is joy; and every place which the goddess deigns to visit is a scene of festivity. No wars are undertaken; arms are untouched; and every hostile weapon is shut up. Peace abroad and at home are then only known; then only loved; till at length the same priest reconducts the goddess, satiated with mortal intercourse, to her temple. [218] The chariot, with its curtain, and, if we may believe it, the goddess herself, then undergo ablution in a secret lake. This office is performed by slaves, whom the same lake instantly swallows up. Hence proceeds a mysterious horror; and a holy ignorance of what that can be, which is beheld only by those who are about to perish. This part of the Suevian nation extends to the most remote recesses of Germany.

41. If we now follow the course of the Danube, as we before did that of the Rhine, we first meet with the Hermunduri; [219] a people faithful to the Romans, [220] and on that account the only Germans who are admitted to commerce, not on the bank alone, but within our territories, and in the flourishing colony [221] established in the province of Rhaetia. They pass and repass at pleasure, without being attended by a guard; and while we exhibit to other nations our arms and camps alone, to these we lay open our houses and country seats, which they behold without coveting. In the country of the Hermunduri rises the Elbe; [222] a river formerly celebrated and known among us, now only heard of by name.

42. Contiguous to the Hermunduri are the Narisci; [223] and next to them, the Marcomanni [224] and Quadi. [225] Of these, the Marcomanni are the most powerful and renowned; and have even acquired the country which they inhabit, by their valor in expelling the Boii. [226] Nor are the Narisci and Quadi inferior in bravery; [227] and this is, as it were, the van of Germany as far as it is bordered by the Danube. Within our memory the Marcomanni and Quadi were governed by kings of their own nation, of the noble line of Maroboduus [228] and Tudrus. They now submit even to foreigners; but all the power of their kings depends upon the authority of the Romans. [229] We seldom assist them with our arms, but frequently with our money; nor are they the less potent on that account.

43. Behind these are the Marsigni, [230] Gothini, [231] Osi, [232] and Burrii, [233] who close the rear of the Marcomanni and Quadi. Of these, the Marsigni and Burrii in language [234] and dress resemble the Suevi. The Gothini and Osi prove themselves not to be Germans; the first, by their use of the Gallic, the second, of the

Pannonian tongue; and both, by their submitting to pay tribute: which is levied on them, as aliens, partly by the Sarmatians, partly by the Quadi. The Gothini, to their additional disgrace, work iron mines. [235] All these people inhabit but a small proportion of champaign country; their settlements are chiefly amongst forests, and on the sides and summits of mountains; for a continued ridge of mountains [236] separates Suevia from various remoter tribes. Of these, the Lygian [237] is the most extensive, and diffuses its name through several communities. It will be sufficient to name the most powerful of them—the Arii, Helvecones, Manimi, Elysii, and Naharvali. [238] In the country of the latter is a grove, consecrated to religious rites of great antiquity. A priest presides over them, dressed in woman's apparel; but the gods worshipped there are said, according to the Roman interpretation, to be Castor and Pollux. Their attributes are the same; their name, Alcis. [239] No images, indeed, or vestiges of foreign superstition, appear in their worship; but they are revered under the character of young men and brothers. The Arii, fierce beyond the superiority of strength they possess over the other just enumerated people, improve their natural ferocity of aspect by artificial helps. Their shields are black; their bodies painted: [240] they choose the darkest nights for an attack; and strike terror by the funereal gloom of their sable bands—no enemy being able to sustain their singular, and, as it were, infernal appearance; since in every combat the eyes are the first part subdued. Beyond the Lygii are the Gothones, [241] who live under a monarchy, somewhat more strict than that of the other German nations, yet not to a degree incompatible with liberty. Adjoining to these are the Rugii [242] and Lemovii, [243] situated on the sea-coast—all these tribes are distinguished by round shields, short swords, and submission to regal authority.

44. Next occur the communities of the Suiones, [244] seated in the very Ocean, [245] who, besides their strength in men and arms, also possess a naval force. [246] The form of their vessels differs from ours in having a prow at each end, [247] so that they are always ready to advance. They make no use of sails, nor have regular benches of oars at the sides: they row, as is practised in some rivers, without order, sometimes on one side, sometimes on the other, as occasion requires. These people honor wealth; [248] for which reason they are subject to monarchical government, without any limitations, [249] or precarious conditions of allegiance. Nor are arms allowed to be kept promiscuously, as among the other German nations: but are committed to the charge of a keeper, and he, too, a slave. The men unemployed, with arms in their hands, readily become licentious. In fact, it is for the king's interest not to entrust a noble, a freeman, or even an emancipated slave, with the custody of arms.

45. Beyond the Suiones is another sea, sluggish and almost stagnant, [250] by which the whole globe is imagined to be girt and enclosed, from this circumstance, that the last light of the setting sun continues so vivid till its rising, as to obscure the stars. [251] Popular belief adds, that the sound of his emerging [252] from the ocean is also heard; and the forms of deities, [253] with the rays beaming from his head, are beheld. Only thus far, report says truly, does nature extend. [254] On the right shore of the Suevic sea [255] dwell the tribes of the Aestii, [256] whose dress and customs are the same with those of the Suevi, but their language more resembles the British. [257] They worship the mother of the gods; [258] and as the symbol of their

superstition, they carry about them the figures of wild boars. [250] This serves them in place of armor and every other defence: it renders the votary of the goddess safe even in the midst of foes. Their weapons are chiefly clubs, iron being little used among them. They cultivate corn and other fruits of the earth with more industry than German indolence commonly exerts. [260] They even explore the sea; and are the only people who gather amber, which by them is called *Glese*, [261] and is collected among the shallows and upon the shore. [262] With the usual indifference of barbarians, they have not inquired or ascertained from what natural object or by what means it is produced. It long lay disregarded [263] amidst other things thrown up by the sea, till our luxury [264] gave it a name. Useless to them, they gather it in the rough; bring it unwrought; and wonder at the price they receive. It would appear, however, to be an exudation from certain trees; since reptiles, and even winged animals, are often seen shining through it, which, entangled in it while in a liquid state, became enclosed as it hardened. [264] I should therefore imagine that, as the luxuriant woods and groves in the secret recesses of the East exude frankincense and balsam, so there are the same in the islands and continents of the West; which, acted upon by the near rays of the sun, drop their liquid juices into the subjacent sea, whence, by the force of tempests, they are thrown out upon the opposite coasts. If the nature of amber be examined by the application of fire, it kindles like a torch, with a thick and odorous flame; and presently resolves into a glutinous matter resembling pitch or resin. The several communities of the Sitones [266] succeed those of the Suiones; to whom they are similar in other respects, but differ in submitting to a female reign; so far have they degenerated, not only from liberty, but even from slavery. Here Suevia terminates.

46. I am in doubt whether to reckon the Peucini, Venedi, and Fenni among the Germans or Sarmatians; [267] although the Peucini, [268] who are by some called Bastarnae, agree with the Germans in language, apparel, and habitations. [269] All of them live in filth and laziness. The intermarriages of their chiefs with the Sarmatians have debased them by a mixture of the manners of that people. [270] The Venedi have drawn much from this source; [271] for they overrun in their predatory excursions all the woody and mountainous tracts between the Peucini and Fenni. Yet even these are rather to be referred to the Germans, since they build houses, carry shields, and travel with speed on foot; in all which particulars they totally differ from the Sarmatians, who pass their time in wagons and on horseback. [272] The Fenni [273] live in a state of amazing savageness and squalid poverty. They are destitute of arms, horses, and settled abodes: their food is herbs; [274] their clothing, skins; their bed, the ground. Their only dependence is on their arrows, which, for want of iron, are headed with bone; [275] and the chase is the support of the women as well as the men; the former accompany the latter in the pursuit, and claim a share of the prey. Nor do they provide any other shelter for their infants from wild beasts and storms, than a covering of branches twisted together. This is the resort of youth; this is the receptacle of old age. Yet even this way of life is in their estimation happier than groaning over the plough; toiling in the erection of houses; subjecting their own fortunes and those of others to the agitations of alternate hope and fear. Secure against men, secure against the gods, they have attained the most difficult point, not to need even a wish.

All our further accounts are intermixed with fable; as, that the Hellusii and Oxionae [276] have human faces, with the bodies and limbs of wild beasts. These unauthenticated reports I shall leave untouched. [277]

THE LIFE OF CNAEUS JULIUS AGRICOLA.

[This work is supposed by the commentators to have been written before the treatise on the manners of the Germans, in the third consulship of the emperor Nerva, and the second of Verginius Rufus, in the year of Rome 850, and of the Christian era 97. Brotier accedes to this opinion; but the reason which he assigns does not seem to be satisfactory. He observes that Tacitus, in the third section, mentions the emperor Nerva; but as he does not call him Divus Nerva, the deified Nerva, the learned commentator infers that Nerva was still living. This reasoning might have some weight, if we did not read, in section 44, that it was the ardent wish of Agricola that he might live to behold Trajan in the imperial seat. If Nerva was then alive, the wish to see another in his room would have been an awkward compliment to the reigning prince. It is, perhaps, for this reason that Lipsius thinks this very elegant tract was written at the same time with the Manners of the Germans, in the beginning of the emperor Trajan. The question is not very material, since conjecture alone must decide it. The piece itself is admitted to be a masterpiece in the kind. Tacitus was son-in-law to Agricola; and while filial piety breathes through his work, he never departs from the integrity of his own character. He has left an historical monument highly interesting to every Briton, who wishes to know the manners of his ancestors, and the spirit of liberty that from the earliest time distinguished the natives of Britain. "Agricola," as Hume observes, "was the general who finally established the dominion of the Romans in this island. He governed, it in the reigns of Vespasian, Titus, and Domitian. He carried his victorious arms northward: defeated the Britons in every encounter, pierced into the forests and the mountains of Caledonia, reduced every state to subjection in the southern parts of the island, and chased before him all the men of fiercer and more intractable spirits, who deemed war and death itself less intolerable than servitude under the victors. He defeated them in a decisive action, which they fought under Galgacus; and having fixed a chain of garrisons between the friths of Clyde and Forth, he cut off the ruder and more barren parts of the island, and secured the Roman province from the incursions of the barbarous inhabitants. During these military enterprises he neglected not the arts of peace. He introduced laws and civility among the Britons; taught them to desire and raise all the conveniences of life; reconciled them to the Roman language and manners; instructed them in letters and science; and employed every expedient to render those chains, which he had forged, both easy and agreeable to them." (Hume's Hist. vol. i. p. 9.) In this passage Mr. Hume has given a summary of the Life of Agricola. It is extended by Tacitus in a style more open than the didactic form of the essay on the German Manners required, but still with the precision, both in sentiment and diction, peculiar to the author. In rich but subdued colors he gives a striking picture of Agricola, leaving to posterity a portion of history which it would be in vain to seek in the dry gazette style of Suetonius, or in the page of any writer of that period.]

1. The ancient custom of transmitting to posterity the actions and manners of famous men, has not been neglected even by the present age, incurious though it be about those belonging to it, whenever any exalted and noble degree of virtue has triumphed over that false estimation of merit, and that ill-will to it, by which small and great states are equally infested. In former times, however, as there was a greater

24

propensity and freer scope for the performance of actions worthy of remembrance, so every person of distinguished abilities was induced through conscious satisfaction in the task alone, without regard to private favor or interest, to record examples of virtue. And many considered it rather as the honest confidence of integrity, than a culpable arrogance, to become their own biographers. Of this, Rutilius and Scaurus [1] were instances; who were never yet censured on this account, nor was the fidelity of their narrative called in question; so much more candidly are virtues always estimated; in those periods which are the most favorable to their production. For myself, however, who have undertaken to be the historian of a person deceased, an apology seemed necessary; which I should not have made, had my course lain through times less cruel and hostile to virtue. [2]

2. We read that when Arulenus Rusticus published the praises of Paetus Thrasea, and Herennius Senecio those of Priscus Helvidius, it was construed into a capital crime; [3] and the rage of tyranny was let loose not only against the authors, but against their writings; so that those monuments of exalted genius were burnt at the place of election in the forum by triumvirs appointed for the purpose. In that fire they thought to consume the voice of the Roman people, the freedom of the senate, and the conscious emotions of all mankind; crowning the deed by the expulsion of the professors of wisdom, [4] and the banishment of every liberal art, that nothing generous or honorable might remain. We gave, indeed, a consummate proof of our patience; and as remote ages saw the very utmost degree of liberty, so we, deprived by inquisitions of all the intercourse of conversation, experienced the utmost of slavery. With language we should have lost memory itself, had it been as much in our power to forget, as to be silent.

3. Now our spirits begin to revive. But although at the first dawning of this happy period, [5] the emperor Nerva united two things before incompatible, monarchy and liberty; and Trajan is now daily augmenting the felicity of the empire; and the public security [6] has not only assumed hopes and wishes, but has seen those wishes arise to confidence and stability; yet, from the nature of human infirmity, remedies are more tardy in their operation than diseases; and, as bodies slowly increase, but quickly perish, so it is more easy to suppress industry and genius, than to recall them. For indolence itself acquires a charm; and sloth, however odious at first, becomes at length engaging. During the space of fifteen years, [7] a large portion of human life, how great a number have fallen by casual events, and, as was the fate of all the most distinguished, by the cruelty of the prince; whilst we, the few survivors, not of others alone, but, if I may be allowed the expression, of ourselves, find a void of so many years in our lives, which has silently brought us from youth to maturity, from mature age to the very verge of life! Still, however, I shall not regret having composed, though in rude and artless language, a memorial of past servitude, and a testimony of present blessings. [8]

The present work, in the meantime, which is dedicated to the honor of my father-in-law, may be thought to merit approbation, or at least excuse, from the piety of the intention.

4. *Cnaeus Julius Agricola* was born at the ancient and illustrious colony of Forumjulii. [9] Both his grandfathers were imperial procurators, [10] an office which confers the rank of equestrian nobility. His father, Julius Graecinus, [11] of the senatorian order, was famous for the study of eloquence and philosophy; and by these accomplishments he drew on himself the displeasure of Caius Cæsar; [12] for, being commanded to undertake the accusation of Marcus Silanus, [13]—on his refusal, he was put to death. His mother was Julia Procilla, a lady of exemplary chastity. Educated with tenderness in her bosom, [14] he passed his childhood and youth in the attainment of every liberal art. He was preserved from the allurements of vice, not only by a naturally good disposition, but by being sent very early to pursue his studies at Massilia; [15] a place where Grecian politeness and provincial frugality are happily united. I remember he was used to relate, that in his early youth he should have engaged with more ardor in philosophical speculation than was suitable to a Roman and a senator, had not the prudence of his mother restrained the warmth and vehemence of his disposition: for his lofty and upright spirit, inflamed by the charms of glory and exalted reputation, led him to the pursuit with more eagerness than discretion. Reason and riper years tempered his warmth; and from the study of wisdom, he retained what is most difficult to compass,—moderation.

5. He learned the rudiments of war in Britain, under Suetonius Paullinus, an active and prudent commander, who chose him for his tent companion, in order to form an estimate of his merit. [16] Nor did Agricola, like many young men, who convert military service into wanton pastime, avail himself licentiously or slothfully of his tribunitial title, or his inexperience, to spend his time in pleasures and absences from duty; but he employed himself in gaining a knowledge of the country, making himself known to the army, learning from the experienced, and imitating the best; neither pressing to be employed through vainglory, nor declining it through timidity; and performing his duty with equal solicitude and spirit. At no other time in truth was Britain more agitated or in a state of greater uncertainty. Our veterans slaughtered, our colonies burnt, [17] our armies cut off, [18]—we were then contending for safety, afterwards for victory. During this period, although all things were transacted under the conduct and direction of another, and the stress of the whole, as well as the glory of recovering the province, fell to the general's share, yet they imparted to the young Agricola skill, experience, and incentives; and the passion for military glory entered his soul; a passion ungrateful to the times, [19] in which eminence was unfavorably construed, and a great reputation was no less dangerous than a bad one.

6. Departing thence to undertake the offices of magistracy in Rome, he married Domitia Decidiana, a lady of illustrious descent, from which connection he derived credit and support in his pursuit of greater things. They lived together in admirable harmony and mutual affection; each giving the preference to the other; a conduct equally laudable in both, except that a greater degree of praise is due to a good wife, in proportion as a bad one deserves the greater censure. The lot of quaestorship [20] gave him Asia for his province, and the proconsul Salvius Titianus [21] for his superior; by neither of which circumstances was he corrupted, although the province was wealthy and open to plunder, and the proconsul, from his rapacious disposition, would readily have agreed to a mutual concealment of guilt. His family was there

26

increased by the birth of a daughter, who was both the support of his house, and his consolation; for he lost an elder-born son in infancy. The interval between his serving the offices of quaestor and tribune of the people, and even the year of the latter magistracy, he passed in repose and inactivity; well knowing the temper of the times under Nero, in which indolence was wisdom. He maintained the same tenor of conduct when praetor; for the judiciary part of the office did not fall to his share. [22] In the exhibition of public games, and the idle trappings of dignity, he consulted propriety and the measure of his fortune; by no means approaching to extravagance, yet inclining rather to a popular course. When he was afterwards appointed by Galba to manage an inquest concerning the offerings which had been presented to the temples, by his strict attention and diligence he preserved the state from any further sacrilege than what it had suffered from Nero. [23]

7. The following year [24] inflicted a severe wound on his peace of mind, and his domestic concerns. The fleet of Otho, roving in a disorderly manner on the coast, [25] made a hostile descent on Intemelii, [26] a part of Liguria, in which the mother of Agricola was murdered at her own estate, her lands were ravaged, and a great part of her effects, which had invited the assassins, was carried off. As Agricola upon this event was hastening to perform the duties of filial piety, he was overtaken by the news of Vespasian's aspiring to the empire, [27] and immediately went over to his party. The first acts of power, and the government of the city, were entrusted to Mucianus; Domitian being at that time very young, and taking no other privilege from his father's elevation than that of indulging his licentious tastes. Mucianus, having approved the vigor and fidelity of Agricola in the service of raising levies, gave him the command of the twentieth legion, [28] which had appeared backward in taking the oaths, as soon as he had heard the seditious practices of his commander. [29] This legion had been unmanageable and formidable even to the consular lieutenants; [30] and its late commander, of praetorian rank, had not sufficient authority to keep it in obedience; though it was uncertain whether from his own disposition, or that of his soldiers. Agricola was therefore appointed as his successor and avenger; but, with an uncommon degree of moderation, he chose rather to have it appear that he had found the legion obedient, than that he had made it so.

8. Vettius Bolanus was at that time governor of Britain, and ruled with a milder sway than was suitable to so turbulent a province. Under his administration, Agricola, accustomed to obey, and taught to consult utility as well as glory, tempered his ardor, and restrained his enterprising spirit. His virtues had soon a larger field for their display, from the appointment of Petilius Cerealis, [31] a man of consular dignity, to the government. At first he only shared the fatigues and dangers of his general; but was presently allowed to partake of his glory. Cerealis frequently entrusted him with part of his army as a trial of his abilities; and from the event sometimes enlarged his command. On these occasions, Agricola was never ostentatious in assuming to himself the merit of his exploits; but always, as a subordinate officer, gave the honor of his good fortune to his superior. Thus, by his spirit in executing orders, and his modesty in reporting his success, he avoided envy, yet did not fail of acquiring reputation.

9. On his return from commanding the legion he was raised by Vespasian to the patrician order, and then invested with the government of Aquitania, [32] a distinguished promotion, both in respect to the office itself, and the hopes of the consulate to which it destined him. It is a common supposition that military men, habituated to the unscrupulous and summary processes of camps, where things are carried with a strong hand, are deficient in the address and subtlety of genius requisite in civil jurisdiction. Agricola, however, by his natural prudence, was enabled to act with facility and precision even among civilians. He distinguished the hours of business from those of relaxation. When the court or tribunal demanded his presence, he was grave, intent, awful, yet generally inclined to lenity. When the duties of his office were over, the man of power was instantly laid aside. Nothing of sternness, arrogance, or rapaciousness appeared; and, what was a singular felicity, his affability did not impair his authority, nor his severity render him less beloved. To mention integrity and freedom from corruption in such a man, would be an affront to his virtues. He did not even court reputation, an object to which men of worth frequently sacrifice, by ostentation or artifice: equally avoiding competition with, his colleagues, [33] and contention with the procurators. To overcome in such a contest he thought inglorious; and to be put down, a disgrace. Somewhat less than three years were spent in this office, when he was recalled to the immediate prospect of the consulate; while at the same time a popular opinion prevailed that the government of Britain would he conferred upon him; an opinion not founded upon any suggestions of his own, but upon his being thought equal to the station. Common fame does not always err, sometimes it even directs a choice. When consul, [34] he contracted his daughter, a lady already of the happiest promise, to myself, then a very young man; and after his office was expired I received her in marriage. He was immediately appointed governor of Britain, and the pontificate [35] was added to his other dignities.

10. The situation and inhabitants of Britain have been described by many writers; [36] and I shall not add to the number with the view of vying with them in accuracy and ingenuity, but because it was first thoroughly subdued in the period of the present history. Those things which, while yet unascertained, they embellished with their eloquence, shall here be related with a faithful adherence to known facts. Britain, the largest of all the islands which have come within the knowledge of the Romans, stretches on the east towards Germany, on the west towards Spain, [37] and on the south it is even within sight of Gaul. Its northern extremity has no opposite land, but is washed by a wide and open sea. Livy, the most eloquent of ancient, and Fabius Rusticus, of modern writers, have likened the figure of Britain to an oblong target, or a two-edged axe. [38] And this is in reality its appearance, exclusive of Caledonia; whence it has been popularly attributed to the whole island. But that tract of country, irregularly stretching out to an immense length towards the furthest shore, is gradually contracted in form of a wedge. [39] The Roman fleet, at this period first sailing round this remotest coast, gave certain proof that Britain was an island; and at the same time discovered and subdued the Orcades, [40] islands till then unknown. Thule [41] was also distinctly seen, which winter and eternal snow had hitherto concealed. The sea is reported to be sluggish and laborious to the rower; and even to be scarcely agitated by winds. The cause of this stagnation I imagine to be the deficiency of land and mountains where tempests are generated;

and the difficulty with which such a mighty mass of waters, in an uninterrupted main, is put in motion. [42] It is not the business of this work to investigate the nature of the ocean and the tides; a subject which many writers have already undertaken. I shall only add one circumstance: that the dominion of the sea is nowhere more extensive; that it carries many currents in this direction and in that; and its ebbings and flowings are not confined to the shore, but it penetrates into the heart of the country, and works its way among hills and mountains, as though it were in its own domain. [43]

11. Who were the first inhabitants of Britain, whether indigenous [44] or immigrants, is a question involved in the obscurity usual among barbarians. Their temperament of body is various, whence deductions are formed of their different origin. Thus, the ruddy hair and large limbs of the Caledonians [45] point out a German derivation. The swarthy complexion and curled hair of the Silures, [46] together with their situation opposite to Spain, render it probable that a colony of the ancient Iberi [47] possessed themselves of that territory. They who are nearest Gaul [48] resemble the inhabitants of that country; whether from the duration of hereditary influence, or whether it be that when lands jut forward in opposite directions, [49] climate gives the same condition of body to the inhabitants of both. On a general survey, however, it appears probable that the Gauls originally took possession of the neighboring coast. The sacred rites and superstitions [50] of these people are discernible among the Britons. The languages of the two nations do not greatly differ. The same audacity in provoking danger, and irresolution in facing it when present, is observable in both. The Britons, however, display more ferocity, [51] not being yet softened by a long peace: for it appears from history that the Gauls were once renowned in war, till, losing their valor with their liberty, languor and indolence entered amongst them. The same change has also taken place among those of the Britons who have been long subdued; [52] but the rest continue such as the Gauls formerly were.

12. Their military strength consists in infantry; some nations also make use of chariots in war; in the management of which, the most honorable person guides the reins, while his dependents fight from the chariot. [53] The Britons were formerly governed by kings, [54] but at present they are divided in factions and parties among their chiefs; and this want of union for concerting some general plan is the most favorable circumstance to us, in our designs against so powerful a people. It is seldom that two or three communities concur in repelling the common danger; and thus, while they engage singly, they are all subdued. The sky in this country is deformed by clouds and frequent rains; but the cold is never extremely rigorous. [55] The length of the days greatly exceeds that in our part of the world. [56] The nights are bright, and, at the extremity of the island, so short, that the close and return of day is scarcely distinguished by a perceptible interval. It is even asserted that, when clouds do not intervene, the splendor of the sun is visible during the whole night, and that it does not appear to rise and set, but to move across. [57] The cause of this is, that the extreme and flat parts of the earth, casting a low shadow, do not throw up the darkness, and so night falls beneath the sky and the stars. [58] The soil, though improper for the olive, the vine, and other productions of warmer climates, is fertile, and suitable for corn. Growth is quick, but maturation slow; both from the same

cause, the great humidity of the ground and the atmosphere. [59] The earth yields gold and silver [60] and other metals, the rewards of victory. The ocean produces pearls, [61] but of a cloudy and livid hue; which some impute to unskilfulness in the gatherers; for in the Red Sea the fish are plucked from the rocks alive and vigorous, but in Britain they are collected as the sea throws them up. For my own part, I can more readily conceive that the defect is in the nature of the pearls, than in our avarice.

13. The Britons cheerfully submit to levies, tributes, and the other services of government, if they are not treated injuriously; but such treatment they bear with impatience, their subjection only extending to obedience, not to servitude. Accordingly Julius Cæsar, [62] the first Roman who entered Britain with an army, although he terrified the inhabitants by a successful engagement, and became master of the shore, may be considered rather to have transmitted the discovery than the possession of the country to posterity. The civil wars soon succeeded; the arms of the leaders were turned against their country; and a long neglect of Britain ensued, which continued even after the establishment of peace. This Augustus attributed to policy; and Tiberius to the injunctions of his predecessor. [63] It is certain that Caius Cæsar [64] meditated an expedition into Britain; but his temper, precipitate in forming schemes, and unsteady in pursuing them, together with the ill success of his mighty attempts against Germany, rendered the design abortive. Claudius [65] accomplished the undertaking, transporting his legions and auxiliaries, and associating Vespasian in the direction of affairs, which laid the foundation of his future fortune. In this expedition, nations were subdued, kings made captive, and Vespasian was held forth to the fates.

14. Aulus Plautius, the first consular governor, and his successor, Ostorius Scapula, [66] were both eminent for military abilities. Under them, the nearest part of Britain was gradually reduced into the form of a province, and a colony of veterans [67] was settled. Certain districts were bestowed upon king Cogidunus, a prince who continued in perfect fidelity within our own memory. This was done agreeably to the ancient and long established practice of the Romans, to make even kings the instruments of servitude. Didius Gallus, the next governor, preserved the acquisitions of his predecessors, and added a very few fortified posts in the remoter parts, for the reputation of enlarging his province. Veranius succeeded, but died within the year. Suetonius Paullinus then commanded with success for two years, subduing various nations, and establishing garrisons. In the confidence with which this inspired him, he undertook an expedition against the island Mona, [68] which had furnished the revolters with supplies; and thereby exposed the settlements behind him to a surprise.

15. For the Britons, relieved from present dread by the absence of the governor, began to hold conferences, in which they painted the miseries of servitude, compared their several injuries, and inflamed each other with such representations as these: "That the only effects of their patience were more grievous impositions upon a people who submitted with such facility. Formerly they had one king respectively; now two were set over them, the lieutenant and the procurator, the former of whom

vented his rage upon their life's blood, the latter upon their properties; [69] the union or discord [70] of these governors was equally fatal to those whom they ruled, while the officers of the one, and the centurions of the other, joined in oppressing them by all kinds of violence and contumely; so that nothing was exempted from their avarice, nothing from their lust. In battle it was the bravest who took spoils; but those whom *they* suffered to seize their houses, force away their children, and exact levies, were, for the most part, the cowardly and effeminate; as if the only lesson of suffering of which they were ignorant was how to die for their country. Yet how inconsiderable would the number of invaders appear did the Britons but compute their own forces! From considerations like these, Germany had thrown off the yoke, [71] though a river [72] and not the ocean was its barrier. The welfare of their country, their wives, and their parents called them to arms, while avarice and luxury alone incited their enemies; who would withdraw as even the deified Julius had done, if the present race of Britons would emulate the valor of their ancestors, and not be dismayed at the event of the first or second engagement. Superior spirit and perseverence were always the share of the wretched; and the gods themselves now seemed to compassionate the Britons, by ordaining the absence of the general, and the detention of his army in another island. The most difficult point, assembling for the purpose of deliberation, was already accomplished; and there was always more danger from the discovery of designs like these, than from their execution."

16. Instigated by such suggestions, they unanimously rose in arms, led by Boadicea, [73] a woman of royal descent (for they make no distinction between the sexes in succession to the throne), and attacking the soldiers dispersed through the garrisons, stormed the fortified posts, and invaded the colony [74] itself, as the seat of slavery. They omitted no species of cruelty with which rage and victory could inspire barbarians; and had not Paullinus, on being acquainted with the commotion of the province, marched speedily to its relief, Britain would have been lost. The fortune of a single battle, however, reduced it to its former subjection; though many still remained in arms, whom the consciousness of revolt, and particular dread of the governor, had driven to despair. Paullinus, although otherwise exemplary in his administration, having treated those who surrendered with severity, and having pursued too rigorous measures, as one who was revenging his own personal injury also, Petronius Turpilianus [75] was sent in his stead, as a person more inclined to lenity, and one who, being unacquainted with the enemy's delinquency, could more easily accept their penitence. After having restored things to their former quiet state, he delivered the command to Trebellius Maximus. [76] Trebellius, indolent, and inexperienced in military affairs, maintained the tranquillity of the province by popular manners; for even the barbarians had now learned to pardon under the seductive influence of vices; and the intervention of the civil wars afforded a legitimate excuse for his inactivity. Sedition however infected the soldiers, who, instead of their usual military services, were rioting in idleness. Trebellius, after escaping the fury of his army by flight and concealment, dishonored and abased, regained a precarious authority; and a kind of tacit compact took place, of safety to the general, and licentiousness to the army. This mutiny was not attended with bloodshed. Vettius Bolanus, [77] succeeding during the continuance of the civil wars, was unable to introduce discipline into Britain. The same inaction towards the enemy, and the same insolence in the camp, continued; except that Bolanus,

unblemished in his character, and not obnoxious by any crime, in some measure substituted affection in the place of authority.

17. At length, when Vespasian received the possession of Britain together with the rest of the world, the great commanders and well-appointed armies which were sent over abated the confidence of the enemy; and Petilius Cerealis struck terror by an attack upon the Brigantes, [78] who are reputed to compose the most populous state in the whole province. Many battles were fought, some of them attended with much bloodshed; and the greater part of the Brigantes were either brought into subjection, or involved in the ravages of war. The conduct and reputation of Cerealis were so brilliant that they might have eclipsed the splendor of a successor; yet Julius Frontinus, [79] a truly great man, supported the arduous competition, as far as circumstances would permit. [80] He subdued the strong and warlike nation of the Silures, [81] in which expedition, besides the valor of the enemy, he had the difficulties of the country to struggle with.

18. Such was the state of Britain, and such had been the vicissitudes of warfare, when Agricola arrived in the middle of summer; [82] at a time when the Roman soldiers, supposing the expeditions of the year were concluded, were thinking of enjoying themselves without care, and the natives, of seizing the opportunity thus afforded them. Not long before his arrival, the Ordovices [83] had cut off almost an entire corps of cavalry stationed on their frontiers; and the inhabitants of the province being thrown into a state of anxious suspense by this beginning, inasmuch as war was what they wished for, either approved of the example, or waited to discover the disposition of the new governor. [84] The season was now far advanced, the troops dispersed through the country, and possessed with the idea of being suffered to remain inactive during the rest of the year; circumstances which tended to retard and discourage any military enterprise; so that it was generally thought most advisable to be contented with defending the suspected posts: yet Agricola determined to march out and meet the approaching danger. For this purpose, he drew together the detachments from the legions, [85] and a small body of auxiliaries; and when he perceived that the Ordovices would not venture to descend into the plain, he led an advanced party in person to the attack, in order to inspire the rest of his troops with equal ardor. The result of the action was almost the total extirpation of the Ordovices; when Agricola, sensible that renown must be followed up, and that the future events of the war would be determined by the first success, resolved to make an attempt upon the island Mona, from the occupation of which Paullinus had been summoned by the general rebellion of Britain, as before related. [86] The usual deficiency of an unforeseen expedition appearing in the want of transport vessels, the ability and resolution of the general were exerted to supply this defect. A select body of auxiliaries, disencumbered of their baggage, who were well acquainted with the fords, and accustomed, after the manner of their country, to direct their horses and manage their arms while swimming, [87] were ordered suddenly to plunge into the channel; by which movement, the enemy, who expected the arrival of a fleet, and a formal invasion by sea, were struck with terror and astonishment, conceiving nothing arduous or insuperable to troops who thus advanced to the attack. They were therefore induced to sue for peace, and make a surrender of the island; an event which threw lustre on the name of Agricola, who, on the very entrance upon his

province, had employed in toils and dangers that time which is usually devoted to ostentatious parade, and the compliments of office. Nor was he tempted, in the pride of success, to term that an expedition or a victory; which was only bridling the vanquished; nor even to announce his success in laureate despatches. [88] But this concealment of his glory served to augment it; since men were led to entertain a high idea of the grandeur of his future views, when such important services were passed over in silence.

19. Well acquainted with the temper of the province, and taught by the experience of former governors how little proficiency had been made by arms, when success was followed by injuries, he next undertook to eradicate the causes of war. And beginning with himself, and those next to him, he first laid restrictions upon his own household, a task no less arduous to most governors than the administration of the province. He suffered no public business to pass through the hands of his slaves or freedmen. In admitting soldiers into regular service, [89] to attendance about his person, he was not influenced by private favor, or the recommendation or solicitation of the centurions, but considered the best men as likely to prove the most faithful. He would know everything; but was content to let some things pass unnoticed. [90] He could pardon small faults, and use severity to great ones; yet did not always punish, but was frequently satisfied with penitence. He chose rather to confer offices and employments upon such as would not offend, than to condemn those who had offended. The augmentation [91] of tributes and contributions he mitigated by a just and equal assessment, abolishing those private exactions which were more grievous to be borne than the taxes themselves. For the inhabitants had been compelled in mockery to sit by their own locked-up granaries, to buy corn needlessly, and to sell it again at a stated price. Long and difficult journeys had also been imposed upon them; for the several districts, instead of being allowed to supply the nearest winter quarters, were forced to carry their corn to remote and devious places; by which means, what was easy to be procured by all, was converted into an article of gain to a few.

20. By suppressing these abuses in the first year of his administration, he established a favorable idea of peace, which, through the negligence or oppression of his predecessors, had been no less dreaded than war. At the return of summer [92] he assembled his army. On their march, he commended the regular and orderly, and restrained the stragglers; he marked out the encampments, [93] and explored in person the estuaries and forests. At the same time he perpetually harassed the enemy by sudden incursions; and, after sufficiently alarming them, by an interval of forbearance, he held to their view the allurements of peace. By this management, many states, which till that time had asserted their independence, were now induced to lay aside their animosity, and to deliver hostages. These districts were surrounded with castles and forts, disposed with so much attention and judgment, that no part of Britain, hitherto new to the Roman arms, escaped unmolested.

21. The succeeding winter was employed in the most salutary measures. In order, by a taste of pleasures, to reclaim the natives from that rude and unsettled state which prompted them to war, and reconcile them to quiet and tranquillity, he incited

them, by private instigations and public encouragements, to erect temples, courts of justice, and dwelling-houses. He bestowed commendations upon those who were prompt in complying with his intentions, and reprimanded such as were dilatory; thus promoting a spirit of emulation which had all the force of necessity. He was also attentive to provide a liberal education for the sons of their chieftains, preferring the natural genius of the Britons to the attainments of the Gauls; and his attempts were attended with such success, that they who lately disdained to make use of the Roman language, were now ambitious of becoming eloquent. Hence the Roman habit began to be held in honor, and the toga was frequently worn. At length they gradually deviated into a taste for those luxuries which stimulate to vice; porticos, and baths, and the elegancies of the table; and this, from their inexperience, they termed politeness, whilst, in reality, it constituted a part of their slavery.

22. The military expeditions of the third year [94] discovered new nations to the Romans, and their ravages extended as far as the estuary of the Tay. [95] The enemies were thereby struck with such terror that they did not venture to molest the army though harassed by violent tempests; so that they had sufficient opportunity for the erection of fortresses. [96] Persons of experience remarked, that no general had ever shown greater skill in the choice of advantageous situations than Agricola; for not one of his fortified posts was either taken by storm, or surrendered by capitulation. The garrisons made frequent sallies; for they were secured against a blockade by a year's provision in their stores. Thus the winter passed without alarm, and each garrison proved sufficient for its own defence; while the enemy, who were generally accustomed to repair the losses of the summer by the successes of the winter, now equally unfortunate in both seasons, were baffled and driven to despair. In these transactions, Agricola never attempted to arrogate to himself the glory of others; but always bore an impartial testimony to the meritorious actions of his officers, from the centurion to the commander of a legion. He was represented by some as rather harsh in reproof; as if the same disposition which made him affable to the deserving, had inclined him to austerity towards the worthless. But his anger left no relics behind; his silence and reserve were not to be dreaded; and he esteemed it more honorable to show marks of open displeasure, than to entertain secret hatred.

23. The fourth summer [97] was spent in securing the country which had been overrun; and if the valor of the army and the glory of the Roman name had permitted it, our conquests would have found a limit within Britain itself. For the tides of the opposite seas, flowing very far up the estuaries of Clota and Bodotria, [98] almost intersect the country; leaving only a narrow neck of land, which was then defended by a chain of forts. [99] Thus all the territory on this side was held in subjection, and the remaining enemies were removed, as it were, into another island.

24. In the fifth campaign, [100] Agricola, crossing over in the first ship, [101] subdued, by frequent and successful engagements, several nations till then unknown; and stationed troops in that part of Britain which is opposite to Ireland, rather with a view to future advantage, than from any apprehension of danger from that quarter. For the possession of Ireland, situated between Britain and Spain, and lying commodiously to the Gallic sea, [102] would have formed a very beneficial

connection between the most powerful parts of the empire. This island is less than Britain, but larger than those of our sea. [103] Its soil, climate, and the manners and dispositions of its inhabitants, are little different from those of Britain. Its ports and harbors are better known, from the concourse of merchants for the purposes of commerce. Agricola had received into his protection one of its petty kings, who had been expelled by a domestic sedition; and detained him, under the semblance of friendship, till an occasion should offer of making use of him. I have frequently heard him assert, that a single legion and a few auxiliaries would be sufficient entirely to conquer Ireland and keep it in subjection; and that such an event would also have contributed to restrain the Britons, by awing them with the prospect of the Roman arms all around them, and, as it were, banishing liberty from their sight.

25. In the summer which began the sixth year [104] of Agricola's administration, extending his views to the countries situated beyond Bodotria, [105] as a general insurrection of the remoter nations was apprehended, and the enemy's army rendered marching unsafe, he caused the harbors to be explored by his fleet, which, now first acting in aid of the land-forces gave the formidable spectacle of war at once pushed on by sea and land. The cavalry, infantry, and marines were frequently mingled in the same camp, and recounted with mutual pleasure their several exploits and adventures; comparing, in the boastful language of military men, the dark recesses of woods and mountains, with the horrors of waves and tempests; and the land and enemy subdued, with the conquered ocean. It was also discovered from the captives, that the Britons had been struck with consternation at the view of the fleet, conceiving the last refuge of the vanquished to be cut off, now the secret retreats of their seas were disclosed. The various inhabitants of Caledonia immediately took up arms, with great preparations, magnified, however, by report, as usual where the truth is unknown; and by beginning hostilities, and attacking our fortresses, they inspired terror as daring to act offensively; insomuch that some persons, disguising their timidity under the mask of prudence, were for instantly retreating on this side the firth, and relinquishing the country rather than waiting to be driven out. Agricola, in the meantime, being informed that the enemy intended to bear down in several bodies, distributed his army into three divisions, that his inferiority of numbers, and ignorance of the country, might not give them an opportunity of surrounding him.

26. When this was known to the enemy, they suddenly changed their design; and making a general attack in the night upon the ninth legion, which was the weakest, [106] in the confusion of sleep and consternation they slaughtered the sentinels, and burst through the intrenchments. They were now fighting within the camp, when Agricola, who had received information of their march from his scouts, and followed close upon their track, gave orders for the swiftest of his horse and foot to charge the enemy's rear. Presently the whole army raised a general shout; and the standards now glittered at the approach of day. The Britons were distracted by opposite dangers; whilst the Romans in the camp resumed their courage, and secure of safety, began to contend for glory. They now in their turns rushed forwards to the attack, and a furious engagement ensued in the gates of the camp; till by the emulous efforts of both Roman armies, one to give assistance, the other to appear not to need it, the

enemy was routed: and had not the woods and marshes sheltered the fugitives, that day would have terminated the war.

27. The soldiers, inspirited by the steadfastness which characterized and the fame which attended this victory, cried out that "nothing could resist their valor; now was the time to penetrate into the heart of Caledonia, and in a continued series of engagements at length to discover the utmost limits of Britain." Those even who had before recommended caution and prudence, were now rendered rash and boastful by success. It is the hard condition of military command, that a share in prosperous events is claimed by all, but misfortunes are imputed to one alone. The Britons meantime, attributing their defeat not to the superior bravery of their adversaries, but to chance, and the skill of the general, remitted nothing of their confidence; but proceeded to arm their youth, to send their wives and children to places of safety, and to ratify the confederacy of their several states by solemn assemblies and sacrifices. Thus the parties separated with minds mutually irritated.

28. During the same summer, a cohort of Usipii, [107] which had been levied in Germany, and sent over into Britain, performed an extremely daring and memorable action. After murdering a centurion and some soldiers who had been incorporated with them for the purpose of instructing them in military discipline, they seized upon three light vessels, and compelled the masters to go on board with them. One of these, however, escaping to shore, they killed the other two upon suspicion; and before the affair was publicly known, they sailed away, as it were by miracle. They were presently driven at the mercy of the waves; and had frequent conflicts, with various success, with the Britons, defending their property from plunder. [108] At length they were reduced to such extremity of distress as to be obliged to feed upon each other; the weakest being first sacrificed, and then such as were taken by lot. In this manner having sailed round the island, they lost their ships through want of skill; and, being regarded as pirates, were intercepted, first by the Suevi, then by the Frisii. Some of them, after being sold for slaves, by the change of masters were brought to the Roman side of the river, [109] and became notorious from the relation of their extraordinary adventures. [110]

29. In the beginning of the next summer, [111] Agricola received a severe domestic wound in the loss of a son, about a year old. He bore this calamity, not with the ostentatious firmness which many have affected, nor yet with the tears and lamentations of feminine sorrow; and war was one of the remedies of his grief. Having sent forwards his fleet to spread its ravages through various parts of the coast, in order to excite an extensive and dubious alarm, he marched with an army equipped for expedition, to which he had joined the bravest of the Britons whose fidelity had been approved by a long allegiance, and arrived at the Grampian hills, where the enemy was already encamped. [112] For the Britons, undismayed by the event of the former action, expecting revenge or slavery, and at length taught that the common danger was to be repelled by union alone, had assembled the strength of all their tribes by embassies and confederacies. Upwards of thirty thousand men in arms were now descried; and the youth, together with those of a hale and vigorous age, renowned in war, and bearing their several honorary decorations, were still

36

flocking in; when Calgacus, [113] the most distinguished for birth and valor among the chieftans, is said to have harangued the multitude, gathering round, and eager for battle, after the following manner:—

30. "When I reflect on the causes of the war, and the circumstances of our situation, I feel a strong persuasion that our united efforts on the present day will prove the beginning of universal liberty to Britain. For we are all undebased by slavery; and there is no land behind us, nor does even the sea afford a refuge, whilst the Roman fleet hovers around. Thus the use of arms, which is at all times honorable to the brave, now offers the only safety even to cowards. In all the battles which have yet been fought, with various success, against the Romans, our countrymen may be deemed to have reposed their final hopes and resources in us: for we, the noblest sons of Britain, and therefore stationed in its last recesses, far from the view of servile shores, have preserved even our eyes unpolluted by the contact of subjection. We, at the furthest limits both of land and liberty, have been defended to this day by the remoteness of our situation and of our fame. The extremity of Britain is now disclosed; and whatever is unknown becomes an object of magnitude. But there is no nation beyond us; nothing but waves and rocks, and the still more hostile Romans, whose arrogance we cannot escape by obsequiousness and submission. These plunderers of the world, after exhausting the land by their devastations, are rifling the ocean: stimulated by avarice, if their enemy be rich; by ambition, if poor; unsatiated by the East and by the West: the only people who behold wealth and indigence with equal avidity. To ravage, to slaughter, to usurp under false titles, they call empire; and where they make a desert, they call it peace. [114]

31. "Our children and relations are by the appointment of nature the dearest of all things to us. These are torn away by levies to serve in foreign lands. [115] Our wives and sisters, though they should escape the violation of hostile force, are polluted under names of friendship and hospitality. Our estates and possessions are consumed in tributes; our grain in contributions. Even our bodies are worn down amidst stripes and insults in clearing woods and draining marshes. Wretches born to slavery are once bought, and afterwards maintained by their masters: Britain every day buys, every day feeds, her own servitude. [116] And as among domestic slaves every new comer serves for the scorn and derision of his fellows; so, in this ancient household of the world, we, as the newest and vilest, are sought out to destruction. For we have neither cultivated lands, nor mines, nor harbors, which can induce them to preserve us for our labors. The valor too and unsubmitting spirit of subjects only render them more obnoxious to their masters; while remoteness and secrecy of situation itself, in proportion as it conduces to security, tends to inspire suspicion. Since then all hopes of mercy are vain, at length assume courage, both you to whom safety and you to whom glory is dear. The Trinobantes, even under a female leader, had force enough to burn a colony, to storm camps, and, if success had not damped their vigor, would have been able entirely to throw off the yoke; and shall not we, untouched, unsubdued, and struggling not for the acquisition but the security of liberty, show at the very first onset what men Caledonia has reserved for her defence?

32. "Can you imagine that the Romans are as brave in war as they are licentious in peace? Acquiring renown from our discords and dissensions, they convert the faults of their enemies to the glory of their own army; an army compounded of the most different nations, which success alone has kept together, and which misfortune will as certainly dissipate. Unless, indeed, you can suppose that Gauls, and Germans, and (I blush to say it) even Britons, who, though they expend their blood to establish a foreign dominion, have been longer its foes than its subjects, will be retained by loyalty and affection! Terror and dread alone are the weak bonds of attachment; which once broken, they who cease to fear will begin to hate. Every incitement to victory is on our side. The Romans have no wives to animate them; no parents to upbraid their flight. Most of them have either no home, or a distant one. Few in number, ignorant of the country, looking around in silent horror at woods, seas, and a heaven itself unknown to them, they are delivered by the gods, as it were imprisoned and bound, into our hands. Be not terrified with an idle show, and the glitter of silver and gold, which can neither protect nor wound. In the very ranks of the enemy we shall find our own bands. The Britons will acknowledge their own cause. The Gauls will recollect their former liberty. The rest of the Germans will desert them, as the Usipii have lately done. Nor is there anything formidable behind them: ungarrisoned forts; colonies of old men; municipal towns distempered and distracted between unjust masters and ill-obeying subjects. Here is a general; here an army. There, tributes, mines, and all the train of punishments inflicted on slaves; which whether to bear eternally, or instantly to revenge, this field must determine. March then to battle, and think of your ancestors and your posterity."

33. They received this harangue with alacrity, and testified their applause after the barbarian manner, with songs, and yells, and dissonant shouts. And now the several divisions were in motion, the glittering of arms was beheld, while the most daring and impetuous were hurrying to the front, and the line of battle was forming; when Agricola, although his soldiers were in high spirits, and scarcely to be kept within their intrenchments, kindled additional ardor by these words:—

"It is now the eighth year, my fellow-soldiers, in which, under the high auspices of the Roman empire, by your valor and perseverance you have been conquering Britain. In so many expeditions, in so many battles, whether you have been required to exert your courage against the enemy, or your patient labors against the very nature of the country, neither have I ever been dissatisfied with my soldiers, nor you with your general. In this mutual confidence, we have proceeded beyond the limits of former commanders and former armies; and are now become acquainted with the extremity of the island, not by uncertain rumor, but by actual possession with our arms and encampments. Britain is discovered and subdued. How often on a march, when embarrassed with mountains, bogs and rivers, have I heard the bravest among you exclaim, 'When shall we descry the enemy? when shall we be led to the field of battle?' At length they are unharbored from their retreats; your wishes and your valor have now free scope; and every circumstance is equally propitious to the victor, and ruinous to the vanquished. For, the greater our glory in having marched over vast tracts of land, penetrated forests, and crossed arms of the sea, while advancing towards the foe, the greater will be our danger and difficulty if we should attempt a retreat. We are inferior to our enemies in knowledge of the country, and less able to command supplies of provision; but we have arms in our hands, and in these we have everything. For myself, it has long been my principle, that a retiring general or army is never safe. Hot only, then, are we to reflect that death with honor is preferable to life with ignominy, but to remember that security and glory are seated in the same place. Even to fall in this extremest verge of earth and of nature cannot be thought an inglorious fate.

34. "If unknown nations or untried troops were drawn up against you, I would exhort you from the example of other armies. At present, recollect your own honors, question your own eyes. These are they, who, the last year, attacking by surprise a single legion in the obscurity of the night, were put to flight by a shout: the greatest fugitives of all the Britons, and therefore the longest survivors. As in penetrating woods and thickets the fiercest animals boldly rush on the hunters, while the weak and timorous fly at their very noise; so the bravest of the Britons have long since fallen: the remaining number consists solely of the cowardly and spiritless; whom you see at length within your reach, not because they have stood their ground, but because they are overtaken. Torpid with fear, their bodies are fixed and chained down in yonder field, which to you will speedily be the scene of a glorious and memorable victory. Here bring your toils and services to a conclusion; close a struggle of fifty years [118] with one great day; and convince your country-men, that to the army ought not to be imputed either the protraction of war, or the causes of rebellion."

35. Whilst Agricola was yet speaking, the ardor of the soldiers declared itself; and as soon as he had finished, they burst forth into cheerful acclamations, and instantly flew to arms. Thus eager and impetuous, he formed them so that the centre was occupied by the auxiliary infantry, in number eight thousand, and three thousand horse were spread in the wings. The legions were stationed in the rear, before the intrenchments; a disposition which would render the victory signally glorious, if it were obtained without the expense of Roman blood; and would ensure support if the rest of the army were repulsed. The British troops, for the greater display of their numbers, and more formidable appearance, were ranged upon the rising grounds, so that the first line stood upon the plain, the rest, as if linked together, rose above one another upon the ascent. The charioteers [119] and horsemen filled the middle of the field with their tumult and careering. Then Agricola, fearing from the superior number of the enemy lest he should be obliged to fight as well on his flanks as in front, extended his ranks; and although this rendered his line of battle less firm, and several of his officers advised him to bring up the legions, yet, filled with hope, and resolute in danger, he dismissed his horse and took his station on foot before the colors.

36. At first the action was carried on at a distance. The Britons, armed with long swords and short targets, [120] with steadiness and dexterity avoided or struck down our missile weapons, and at the same time poured in a torrent of their own. Agricola then encouraged three Batavian and two Tungrian [121] cohorts to fall in and come to close quarters; a method of fighting familiar to these veteran soldiers, but embarrassing to the enemy from the nature of their armor; for the enormous British

swords, blunt at the point, are unfit for close grappling, and engaging in a confined space. When the Batavians; therefore, began to redouble their blows, to strike with the bosses of their shields, and mangle the faces of the enemy; and, bearing down all those who resisted them on the plain, were advancing their lines up the ascent; the other cohorts, fired with ardor and emulation, joined in the charge, and overthrew all who came in their way: and so great was their impetuosity in the pursuit of victory, that they left many of their foes half dead or unhurt behind them. In the meantime the troops of cavalry took to flight, and the armed chariots mingled in the engagement of the infantry; but although their first shock occasioned some consternation, they were soon entangled among the close ranks of the cohorts, and the inequalities of the ground. Not the least appearance was left of an engagement of cavalry; since the men, long keeping their ground with difficulty, were forced along with the bodies of the horses; and frequently, straggling chariots, and affrighted horses without their riders, flying variously as terror impelled them, rushed obliquely athwart or directly through the lines. [122]

37. Those of the Britons who, yet disengaged from the fight, sat on the summits of the hills, and looked with careless contempt on the smallness of our numbers, now began gradually to descend; and would have fallen on the rear of the conquering troops, had not Agricola, apprehending this very event, opposed four reserved squadron of horse to their attack, which, the more furiously they had advanced, drove them back with the greater celerity. Their project was thus turned against themselves; and the squadrons were ordered to wheel from the front of the battle and fall upon the enemy's rear. A striking and hideous spectacle now appeared on the plain: some pursuing; some striking: some making prisoners, whom they slaughtered as others came in their way. Now, as their several dispositions prompted, crowds of armed Britons fled before inferior numbers, or a few, even unarmed, rushed upon their foes, and offered themselves to a voluntary death. Arms, and carcasses, and mangled limbs, were promiscuously strewed, and the field was dyed in blood. Even among the vanquished were seen instances of rage and valor. When the fugitives approached the woods, they collected, and surrounded the foremost of the pursuers, advancing incautiously, and unacquainted with the country; and had not Agricola, who was everywhere present, caused some strong and lightly-equipped cohorts to encompass the ground, while part of the cavalry dismounted made way through the thickets, and part on horseback scoured the open woods, some disaster would have proceeded from the excess of confidence. But when the enemy saw their pursuers again formed in compact order, they renewed their flight, not in bodies as before, or waiting for their companions, but scattered and mutually avoiding each other; and thus took their way to the most distant and devious retreats. Night and satiety of slaughter put an end to the pursuit. Of the enemy ten thousand were slain: on our part three hundred and sixty fell; among whom was Aulus Atticus, the praefect of a cohort, who, by his juvenile ardor, and the fire of his horse, was borne into the midst of the enemy.

38. Success and plunder contributed to render the night joyful to the victors; whilst the Britons, wandering and forlorn, amid the promiscuous lamentations of men and women, were dragging along the wounded; calling out to the unhurt; abandoning their habitations, and in the rage of despair setting them on fire; choosing places of

concealment, and then deserting them; consulting together, and then separating. Sometimes, on beholding the dear pledges of kindred and affection, they were melted into tenderness, or more frequently roused into fury; insomuch that several, according to authentic information, instigated by a savage compassion, laid violent hands upon their own wives and children. On the succeeding day, a vast silence all around, desolate hills, the distant smoke of burning houses, and not a living soul descried by the scouts, displayed more amply the face of victory. After parties had been detached to all quarters without discovering any certain tracks of the enemy's flight, or any bodies of them still in arms, as the lateness of the season rendered it impracticable to spread the war through the country, Agricola led his army to the confines of the Horesti. [123] Having received hostages from this people, he ordered the commander of the fleet to sail round the island; for which expedition he was furnished with sufficient force, and preceded by the terror of the Roman name. Pie himself then led back the cavalry and infantry, marching slowly, that he might impress a deeper awe on the newly conquered nations; and at length distributed his troops into their winter-quarters. The fleet, about the same time, with prosperous gales and renown, entered the Trutulensian [124] harbor, whence, coasting all the hither shore of Britain, it returned entire to its former station. [125]

39. The account of these transactions, although unadorned with the pomp of words in the letters of Agricola, was received by Domitian, as was customary with that prince, with outward expressions of joy, but inward anxiety. He was conscious that his late mock-triumph over Germany, [126] in which he had exhibited purchased slaves, whose habits and hair [127] were contrived to give them the resemblance of captives, was a subject of derision; whereas here, a real and important victory, in which so many thousands of the enemy were slain, was celebrated with universal applause. His greatest dread was that the name of a private man should be exalted above that of the prince. In vain had he silenced the eloquence of the forum, and cast a shade upon all civil honors, if military glory were still in possession of another. Other accomplishments might more easily be connived at, but the talents of a great general were truly imperial. Tortured with such anxious thoughts, and brooding over them in secret, [128] a certain indication of some malignant intention, be judged it most prudent for the present to suspend his rancor, tilt the first burst of glory and the affections of the army should remit: for Agricola still possessed the command in Britain.

40. He therefore caused the senate to decree him triumphal ornaments, [129]—a statue crowned with laurel, and all the other honors which are substituted for a real triumph, together with a profusion of complimentary expressions; and also directed an expectation to be raised that the province of Syria, vacant by the death of Atilius Rufus, a consular man, and usually reserved for persons of the greatest distinction, was designed for Agricola. It was commonly believed that one of the freedmen, who were employed in confidential services, was despatched with the instrument appointing Agricola to the government of Syria, with orders to deliver it if he should be still in Britain; but that this messenger, meeting Agricola in the straits, [130] returned directly to Domitian without so much as accosting him. [131] Whether this was really the fact, or only a fiction founded on the genius and character of the prince, is uncertain. Agricola, in the meantime, had delivered the province, in peace

and security, to his successor; [132] and lest his entry into the city should be rendered too conspicuous by the concourse and acclamations of the people, he declined the salutation of his friends by arriving in the night; and went by night, as he was commanded, to the palace. There, after being received with a slight embrace, but not a word spoken, he was mingled with the servile throng. In this situation, he endeavored to soften the glare of military reputation, which is offensive to those who themselves live in indolence, by the practice of virtues of a different cast. He resigned himself to ease and tranquillity, was modest in his garb and equipage, affable in conversation, and in public was only accompanied by one or two of his friends; insomuch that the many, who are accustomed to form their ideas of great men from their retinue and figure, when they beheld Agricola, were apt to call in question his renown: few could interpret his conduct.

41. He was frequently, during that period, accused in his absence before Domitian, and in his absence also acquitted. The source of his danger was not any criminal action, nor the complaint of any injured person; but a prince hostile to virtue, and his own high reputation, and the worst kind of enemies, eulogists. [133] For the situation of public affairs which ensued was such as would not permit the name of Agricola to rest in silence: so many armies in Moesia, Dacia, Germany, and Pannonia lost through the temerity or cowardice of their generals; [134] so many men of military character, with numerous cohorts, defeated and taken prisoners; whilst a dubious contest was maintained, not for the boundaries, of the empire, and the banks of the bordering rivers, [135] but for the winter-quarters of the legions, and the possession of our territories. In this state of things, when loss succeeded loss, and every year was signalized by disasters and slaughters, the public voice loudly demanded Agricola for general: every one comparing his vigor, firmness, and experience in war, with the indolence and pusillanimity of the others. It is certain that the ears of Domitian himself were assailed by such discourses, while the best of his freedmen pressed him to the choice through motives of fidelity and affection, and the worst through envy and malignity, emotions to which he was of himself sufficiently prone. Thus Agricola, as well by his own virtues as the vices of others, was urged on precipitously to glory.

42. The year now arrived in which the proconsulate of Asia or Africa must fall by lot upon Agricola; [136] and as Civica had lately been put to death, Agricola was not unprovided with a lesson, nor Domitian with an example. [137] Some persons, acquainted with the secret inclinations of the emperor, came to Agricola, and inquired whether he intended to go to his province; and first, somewhat distantly, began to commend a life of leisure and tranquillity; then offered their services in procuring him to be excused from the office; and at length, throwing off all disguise, after using arguments both to persuade and intimidate him, compelled him to accompany them to Domitian. The emperor, prepared to dissemble, and assuming an air of stateliness, received his petition for excuse, and suffered himself to be formally thanked [138] for granting it, without blushing at so invidious a favor. He did not, however, bestow on Agricola the salary [139] usually offered to a proconsul, and which he himself had granted to others; either taking offence that it was not requested, or feeling a consciousness that it would seem a bribe for what he had in reality extorted by his authority. It is a principle of human nature to hate those

whom we have injured; [140] and Domitian was constitutionally inclined to anger, which was the more difficult to be averted, in proportion as it was the more disguised. Yet he was softened by the temper and prudence of Agricola; who did not think it necessary, by a contumacious spirit, or a vain ostentation of liberty, to challenge fame or urge his fate. [141] Let those be apprised, who are accustomed to admire every opposition to control, that even under a bad prince men may be truly great; that submission and modesty, if accompanied with vigor and industry, will elevate a character to a height of public esteem equal to that which many, through abrupt and dangerous paths, have attained, without benefit to their country, by an ambitious death.

43. His decease was a severe affliction to his family, a grief to his friends, and a subject of regret even to foreigners, and those who had no personal knowledge of him. [142] The common people too, and the class who little interest themselves about public concerns, were frequent in their inquiries at his house during his sickness, and made him the subject of conversation at the forum and in private circles; nor did any person either rejoice at the news of his death, or speedily forget it. Their commiseration was aggravated by a prevailing report that he was taken off by poison. I cannot venture to affirm anything certain of this matter; [143] yet, during the whole course of his illness, the principal of the imperial freedmen and the most confidential of the physicians was sent much more frequently than was customary with a court whose visits were chiefly paid by messages; whether that was done out of real solicitude, or for the purposes of state inquisition. On the day of his decease, it is certain that accounts of his approaching dissolution were every instant transmitted to the emperor by couriers stationed for the purpose; and no one believed that the information, which so much pains was taken to accelerate, could be received with regret. He put on, however, in his countenance and demeanor, the semblance of grief: for he was now secured from an object of hatred, and could more easily conceal his joy than his fear. It was well known that on reading the will, in which he was nominated co-heir [144] with the excellent wife and most dutiful daughter of Agricola, he expressed great satisfaction, as if it had been a voluntary testimony of honor and esteem: so blind and corrupt had his mind been rendered by continual adulation, that he was ignorant none but a bad prince could be nominated heir to a good father.

44. Agricola was born in the ides of June, during the third consulate of Caius Cæsar; [145] he died in his fifty-sixth year, on the tenth of the calends of September, when Collega and Priscus were consuls. [146] Posterity may wish to form an idea of his person. His figure was comely rather than majestic. In his countenance there was nothing to inspire awe; its character was gracious and engaging. You would readily have believed him a good man, and willingly a great one. And indeed, although he was snatched away in the midst of a vigorous age, yet if his life be measured by his glory, it was a period of the greatest extent. For after the full enjoyment of all that is truly good, which is found in virtuous pursuits alone, decorated with consular and triumphal ornaments, what more could fortune contribute to his elevation? Immoderate wealth did not fall to his share, yet he possessed a decent affluence. [147] His wife and daughter surviving, his dignity unimpaired, his reputation flourishing, and his kindred and friends yet in safety, it may even be thought an

additional felicity that he was thus withdrawn from impending evils. For, as we have heard him express his wishes of continuing to the dawn of the present auspicious day, and beholding Trajan in the imperial seat,—wishes in which he formed a certain presage of the event; so it is a great consolation, that by his untimely end he escaped that latter period, in which Domitian, not by intervals and remissions, but by a continued, and, as it were, a single act, aimed at the destruction of the commonwealth. [148]

45. Agricola did not behold the senate-house besieged, and the senators enclosed by a circle of arms; [149] and in one havoc the massacre of so many consular men, the flight and banishment of so many honorable women. As yet Carus Metius [150] was distinguished only by a single victory; the counsels of Messalinus [151] resounded only through the Albanian citadel; [152] and Massa Baebius [153] was himself among the accused. Soon after, our own hands [154] dragged Helvidius [155] to prison; ourselves were tortured with the spectacle of Mauricus and Rusticus, [156] and sprinkled with the innocent blood of Senecio. [157]

Even Nero withdrew his eyes from the cruelties he commanded. Under Domitian, it was the principal part of our miseries to behold and to be beheld: when our sighs were registered; and that stern countenance, with its settled redness, [158] his defence against shame, was employed in noting the pallid horror of so many spectators. Happy, O Agricola! not only in the splendor of your life, but in the seasonableness of your death. With resignation and cheerfulness, from the testimony of those who were present in your last moments, did you meet your fate, as if striving to the utmost of your power to make the emperor appear guiltless. But to myself and your daughter, besides the anguish of losing a parent, the aggravating affliction remains, that it was not our lot to watch over your sick-bed, to support you when languishing, and to satiate ourselves with beholding and embracing you. With what attention should we have received your last instructions, and engraven them on our hearts! This is our sorrow; this is our wound: to us you were lost four years before by a tedious absence. Everything, doubtless, O best of parents! was administered for your comfort and honor, while a most affectionate wife sat beside you; yet fewer tears were shed upon your bier, and in the last light which your eyes beheld, something was still wanting.

46. If there be any habitation for the shades of the virtuous; if, as philosophers suppose, exalted souls do not perish with the body; may you repose in peace, and call us, your household, from vain regret and feminine lamentations, to the contemplation of your virtues, which allow no place for mourning or complaining! Let us rather adorn your memory by our admiration, by our short-lived praises, and, as far as our natures will permit, by an imitation of your example. This is truly to honor the dead; this is the piety of every near relation. I would also recommend it to the wife and daughter of this great man, to show their veneration of a husband's and a father's memory by revolving his actions and words in their breasts, and endeavoring to retain an idea of the form and features of his mind, rather than of his person. Not that I would reject those resemblances of the human figure which are engraven in brass or marbles but as their originals are frail and perishable, so likewise are they:

while the form of the mind is eternal, and not to be retained or expressed by any foreign matter, or the artist's skill, but by the manners of the survivors. Whatever in Agricola was the object of our love, of our admiration, remains, and will remain in the minds of men, transmitted in the records of fame, through an eternity of years. For, while many great personages of antiquity will be involved in a common oblivion with the mean and inglorious, Agricola shall survive, represented and consigned to future ages.

FOOTNOTES

A TREATISE ON THE SITUATION, MANNERS AND INHABITANTS OF GERMANY.

[1] This treatise was written in the year of Rome 851, A.D. 98; during the fourth consulate of the emperor Nerva, and the third of Trajan.

[2] The Germany here meant is that beyond the Rhine. The Germania Cisrhenana, divided into the Upper and Lower, was a part of Gallia Belgica.

[3] Rhaetia comprehended the country of the Grisons, with part of Suabia and Bavaria.

[4] Lower Hungary, and part of Austria.

[5] The Carpathian mountains in Upper Hungary.

[6] "Broad promontories." Latos sinus. Sinus strictly signifies "a bending," especially inwards. Hence it is applied to a gulf, or bay, of the sea. And hence, again, by metonymy, to that projecting part of the land, whereby the gulf is formed; and still further to any promontory or peninsula. It is in this latter force it is here used;—and refers especially to the Danish peninsula. See Livy xxvii, 30, xxxviii. 5; Servius on Virgil, Aen. xi. 626.

[7] Scandinavia and Finland, of which the Romans had a very slight knowledge, were supposed to be islands.

[8] The mountains of the Grisons. That in which the Rhine rises is at present called Vogelberg.

[9] Now called Schwartzwald, or the Black Forest. The name Danubius was given to that portion of the river which is included between its source and Vindobona (Vienna); throughout the rest of its course it was called Ister.

[10] *Donec erumpat.* The term *erumpat* is most correctly and graphically employed; for the Danube discharges its waters into the Euxine with so great force, that its course may be distinctly traced for miles out to sea.

[11] There are now but five.

[12] The ancient writers called all nations *indigenae* (*i.e.* inde geniti), or *autochthones*, "sprung from the soil," of whose origin they were ignorant.

[13] It is, however, well established that the ancestors of the Germans migrated by land from Asia. Tacitus here falls into a very common kind of error, in assuming a local fact (viz. the manner in which migrations took place in the basin of the Mediterranean) to be the expression of a general law.—ED.

[14] Drusus, father of the emperor Claudius, was the first Roman general who navigated the German Ocean. The difficulties and dangers which Germanicus met with from the storms of this sea are related in the Annals, ii. 23.

[15] All barbarous nations, in all ages, have applied verse to the same use, as is still found to be the case among the North American Indians. Charlemagne, as we are told by Eginhart, "wrote out and committed to memory barbarous verses of great antiquity, in which the actions and wars of ancient kings were recorded."

[16] The learned Leibnitz supposes this Tuisto to have been the Teut or Teutates so famous throughout Gaul and Spain, who was a Celto-Scythian king or hero, and subdued and civilized a great part of Europe and Asia. Various other conjectures have been formed concerning him and his son Mannus, but most of them extremely vague and improbable. Among the rest, it has been thought that in Mannus and his three sons an obscure tradition is preserved of Adam, and his sons Cain, Abel, and Seth; or of Noah, and his sons Shem, Ham, and Japhet.

[17] Conringius interprets the names of the sons of Mannus into Ingff, Istf, and Hermin.

[18] Pliny, iv. 14, embraces a middle opinion between these, and mentions five capital tribes. The Vindili, to whom belong the Burgundiones, Varini, Carini, and Guttones; the Ingaevones, including the Cimbri, Teutoni, and Chauci; the Istaevones, near the Rhine, part of whom are the midland Cimbri; the Hermiones, containing the Suevi, Hermunduri, Catti, and Cherusci; and the Peucini and Bastarnae, bordering upon the Dacians.

[19] The Marsi appear to have occupied various portions of the northwest part of Germany at various times. In the time of Tiberius (A.D. 14) they sustained a great slaughter from the forces of Germanicus, who ravaged their country for fifty miles with fire and sword, sparing neither age nor sex, neither things profane nor sacred. (See Ann. i. 51.) At this period they were occupying the country in the neighborhood of the Rura (Ruhr), a tributary of the Rhine. Probably this slaughter was the destruction of them as a separate people; and by the time that Trajan succeeded to the imperial power they seem to have been blotted out from amongst the Germanic tribes. Hence their name will not be found in the following account of Germany.

[20] These people are mentioned by Strabo, vii. 1, 3. Their locality is not very easy to determine.

[21] See note, c. 38.

[22] The Vandals are said to have derived their name from the German word *wendeln*, "to wander." They began to be troublesome to the Romans A.D. 160, in the reigns of Aurelius and Verus. In A.D. 410 they made themselves masters of Spain in conjunction with the Alans and Suevi, and received for their share what from them was termed Vandalusia (Andalusia). In A.D. 429 they crossed into Africa under Genseric, who not only made himself master of Byzacium, Gaetulia, and part of Numidia, but also crossed over into Italy, A.D. 455, and plundered Rome. After the death of Genseric the Vandal power declined.

[23] That is, those of the Marsi, Gambrivii, *etc.* Those of Ingaevones, Istaevones, and Hermiones, were not so much names of the people, as terms expressing their situation. For, according to the most learned Germans, the Ingaevones are *die Inwohner*, those dwelling inwards, towards the sea; the Istaevones, *die Westwohner*, the inhabitants of the western parts: and the Hermiones, *die Herumwohner*, the midland inhabitants.

[24] It is however found in an inscription so far back as the year of Rome 531, before Christ 222, recording the victory of Claudius Marcellus over the Galli Insubres and their allies the Germans, at Clastidium, now Chiastezzo in the Milanese.

[25] This is illustrated by a passage in Cæsar, Bell. Gall. ii. 4, where, after mentioning that several of the Belgae were descended from the Germans who had formerly crossed the Rhine and expelled the Gauls, he says, "the first of these emigrants were the Condrusii, Eburones, Caeresi and Paemani, who were called by the common name of Germans." The derivation of German is *Wehr mann*, a warrior, or man of war. This appellation was first used by the victorious Cisrhenane tribes, but not by the whole Transrhenane nation, till they gradually adopted it, as equally due to them on account of their military reputation. The Tungri were formerly a people of great name, the relics of which still exist in the extent of the district now termed the ancient diocese of Tongres.

[26] Under this name Tacitus speaks of some German deity, whose attributes corresponded in the main with those of the Greek and Roman Hercules. What he was called by the Germans is a matter of doubt.—*White*.

[27] *Quem barditum vocant.* The word *barditus* is of Gallic origin, being derived from *bardi*, "bards;" it being a custom with the Gauls for bards to accompany the army, and celebrate the heroic deeds of their great warriors; so that *barditum* would thus signify "the fulfilment of the bard's office." Hence it is clear that *barditum* could not be used correctly here, inasmuch as amongst the Germans not any particular, appointed, body of men, but the whole army chanted forth the war-song. Some editions have *baritum*, which is said to be derived from the German word *beren*, or *baeren*, "to shout;" and hence it is translated in some dictionaries as, "the German war-song." From the following passage extracted from Facciolati, it would seem, however, that German critics repudiate this idea: "De *barito* clamore bellico, seu, ut quaedam habent exemplaria, *bardito*, nihil audiuimus nunc in Germani: nisi hoc dixerimus, qud *bracht*, vel *brecht*, milites Germani appellare consueverunt;

concursum videlicet certantium, et clamorem ad pugnam descendentium; quem *bar, bar, bar*, sonuisse nonnulli affirmant."—(Andr. Althameri, Schol. in C. Tacit De Germanis.) Ritter, himself a German, affirms that *baritus* is a reading worth nothing; and that *barritus* was not the name of the ancient German war-song, but of the shout raised by the Romans in later ages when on the point of engaging; and that it was derived "a clamore barrorem, *i.e.* elephantorum." The same learned editor considers that the words "quem barditum vocant" have been originally the marginal annotation of some unsound scholar, and have been incorporated by some transcriber into the text of his MS. copy, whence the error has spread. He therefore encloses them between brackets, to show that, in his judgment, they are not the genuine production of the pen of Tacitus.— *White*.

[28] A very curious coincidence with the ancient German opinion concerning the prophetic nature of the war-cry or song, appears in the following passage of the Life of Sir Ewen Cameron, in "Pennant's Tour," 1769, Append, p. 363. At the battle of Killicrankie, just before the fight began, "he (Sir Ewen) commanded such of the Camerons as were posted near him to make a great shout, which being seconded by those who stood on the right and left, ran quickly through the whole army, and was returned by the enemy. But the noise of the muskets and cannon, with the echoing of the hills, made the Highlanders fancy that their shouts were much louder and brisker than those of the enemy, and Lochiel cried out, 'Gentlemen, take courage, the day is ours: I am the oldest commander in the army, and have always observed something ominous and fatal in such a dull, hollow and feeble noise as the enemy made in their shout, which prognosticates that they are all doomed to die by our hands this night; whereas ours was brisk, lively and strong, and shows we have vigor and courage.' These words, spreading quickly through the army, animated the troops in a strange manner. The event justified the prediction; the Highlanders obtained a complete victory."

[29] Now Asburg in the county of Meurs.

[30] The Greeks, by means of their colony at Marseilles, introduced their letters into Gaul, and the old Gallic coins have many Greek characters in their inscriptions. The Helvetians also, as we are informed by Cæsar, used Greek letters. Thence they might easily pass by means of commercial intercourse to the neighboring Germans. Count Marsili and others have found monuments with Greek inscriptions in Germany, but not of so early an age.

[31] The large bodies of the Germans are elsewhere taken notice of by Tacitus, and also by other authors. It would appear as if most of them were at that time at least six feet high. They are still accounted some of the tallest people in Europe.

[32] Bavaria and Austria.

[33] The greater degree of cold when the country was overspread with woods and marshes, made this observation more applicable than at present. The same change of temperature from clearing and draining the land has taken place in North America. It

may be added, that the Germans, as we are afterwards informed, paid attention to no kind of culture but that of corn.

[34] The cattle of some parts of Germany are at present remarkably large; so that their former smallness must have rather been owing to want of care in feeding them and protecting them from the inclemencies of winter, and in improving the breed by mixtures, than to the nature of the climate.

[35] Mines both of gold and silver have since been discovered in Germany; the former, indeed, inconsiderable; but the latter, valuable.

[36] As vice and corruption advanced among the Romans, their money became debased and adulterated. Thus Pliny, xxxiii. 3, relates, that "Livius Drusus during his tribuneship, mixed an eighth part of brass with the silver coin;" and ibid. 9, "that Antony the triumvir mixed iron with the denarius: that some coined base metal, others diminished the pieces, and hence it became an art to prove the goodness of the denarii." One precaution for this purpose was cutting the edges like the teeth of a saw, by which means it was seen whether the metal was the same quite through, or was only plated. These were the Serrati, or serrated Denarii. The Bigati were those stamped with the figure of a chariot drawn by two horses, as were the Quadrigati with a chariot and four horses. These were old coin, of purer silver than those of the emperors. Hence the preference of the Germans for certain kinds of species was founded on their apprehension of being cheated with false money.

[37] The Romans had the same predilection for silver coin, and probably on the same account originally. Pliny, in the place above cited, expresses his surprise that "the Roman people had always imposed a tribute in silver on conquered nations; as at the end of the second Punic war, when they demanded an annual payment in silver for fifty years, without any gold."

[38] Iron was in great abundance in the bowels of the earth; but this barbarous people had neither patience, skill, nor industry to dig and work it. Besides, they made use of weapons of stone, great numbers of which are found in ancient tombs and barrows.

[39] This is supposed to take its name from *pfriem* or *priem*, the point of a weapon. Afterwards, when iron grew more plentiful, the Germans chiefly used swords.

[40] It appears, however, from Tacitus's Annals, ii. 14, that the length of these spears rendered them unmanageable in an engagement among trees and bushes.

[41] Notwithstanding the manner of fighting is so much changed in modern times, the arms of the ancients are still in use. We, as well as they, have two kinds of swords, the sharp-pointed, and edged (small sword and sabre). The broad lance subsisted till lately in the halberd; the spear and framea in the long pike and spontoon; the missile weapons in the war hatchet, or North American tomahawk.

50

There are, besides, found in the old German barrows, perforated stone balls, which they threw by means of thongs passed through them.

[42] *Nudi*. The Latin nudus, like the Greek *gemnos*, does not point out a person devoid of all clothing, but merely one without an upper garment— clad merely in a vest or tunic, and that perhaps a short one.—*White*.

[43] This decoration at first denoted the valor, afterwards the nobility, of the bearer; and in process of time gave origin to the armorial ensigns so famous in the ages of chivalry. The shields of the private men were simply colored; those of the chieftains had the figures of animals painted on them.

[44] Plutarch, in his Life of Marius, describes somewhat differently the arms and equipage of the Cimbri. "They wore (says he) helmets representing the heads of wild beasts, and other unusual figures, and crowned with a winged crest, to make them appear taller. They were covered with iron coats of mail, and carried white glittering shields. Each had a battle-axe; and in close fight they used large heavy swords." But the learned Eccard justly observes, that they had procured these arms in their march; for the Holsatian barrows of that age contain few weapons of brass, and none of iron; but stone spear-heads, and instead of swords, the wedgelike bodies vulgarly called thunderbolts.

[46] Casques (*cassis*) are of metal; helmets (*galea*) of leather— *Isidorus*.

[46] This mode of fighting is admirably described by Cæsar. "The Germans engaged after the following manner:—There were 6,000 horse, and an equal number of the swiftest and bravest foot; who were chosen, man by man, by the cavalry, for their protection. By these they were attended in battle; to these they retreated; and, these, if they were hard pressed, joined them in the combat. If any fell wounded from their horses, by these they were covered. If it were necessary to advance or retreat to any considerable distance, such agility had they acquired by exercise, that, supporting themselves by the horses' manes, they kept pace with them."— Bell. Gall. i. 48.

[47] To understand this, it is to be remarked, that the Germans were divided into nations or tribes,—these into cantons, and these into districts or townships. The cantons (*pagi* in Latin) were called by themselves *gauen*. The districts or townships (*vici*) were called *hunderte*, whence the English hundreds. The name given to these select youth, according to the learned Dithmar, was *die hunderte*, hundred men. From the following passage in Cæsar, it appears that in the more powerful tribes a greater number was selected from each canton. "The nation of the Suevi is by far the greatest and most warlike of the Germans. They are said to inhabit a hundred cantons; from each of which a thousand men are sent annually to make war out of their own territories. Thus neither the employments of agriculture, nor the use of arms are interrupted."—Bell. Gall. iv. 1. The warriors were summoned by the *heribannum*, or army-edict; whence is derived the French arrire-ban.

[48] A wedge is described by Vegetius (iii. 19,) as a body of infantry, narrow in front, and widening towards the rear; by which disposition they were enabled to break the enemy's ranks, as all their weapons were directed to one spot. The soldiers called it a boar's head.

[49] It was also considered as the height of injury to charge a person with this unjustly. Thus, by the *Salic* law, tit. xxxiii, 5, a fine of 600 denarii (about 9_l._) is imposed upon "every free man who shall accuse another of throwing down his shield, and running away, without being able to prove it."

[50] Vertot (Mm. de l'Acad. des Inscrip.) supposes that the French *maires du palais* had their origin from these German military leaders. If the kings were equally conspicuous for valor as for birth, they united the regal with the military command. Usually, however, several kings and generals were assembled in their wars. In this case, the most eminent commanded, and obtained a common jurisdiction in war, which did not subsist in time of peace. Thus Cæsar (Bell. Gall. vi.) says, "In peace they have no common magistracy." A general was elected by placing him on a shield, and lifting him on the shoulders of the bystanders. The same ceremonial was observed in the election of kings.

[51] Hence Ambiorix, king of the Eburones, declare that "the nature of his authority was such, that the people had no less power over him, than he over the people."—Cæsar, Bell. Gall. v. The authority of the North American chiefs almost exactly similar.

[52] The power of life and death, however, was in the hands of magistrates. Thus Cæsar: "When a state engages either in an offensive or defensive war, magistrates are chosen to preside over it, and exercise power of life and death."—Bell. Gall. vi. The infliction of punishments was committed to the priests, in order to give them more solemnity, and render them less invidious.

[53] *Effigiesque et signa quaedam.* That effigies does not mean the images of their deities is proved by that is stated at chap. ix., *viz.* that they deemed it derogatory to their deities to represent them in human form; and, if in human form, we may argue, *a fortiori*, in the form of the lower animals. The interpretation of the passage will be best derived from Hist. iv. 22, where Tacitus says:—"Depromptae silvis lucisve ferarum imagines, ut cuique genti inire praelium mos est." It would hence appear that these effigies and signa were images of wild animals, and were national standards preserved with religious care in sacred woods and groves, whence they were brought forth when the clan or tribe was about to take the field.—*White.*

[54] They not only interposed to prevent the flight of their husbands and sons, but, in desperate emergencies, themselves engaged in battle. This happened on Marius's defeat of the Cimbri (hereafter to be mentioned); and Dio relates, that when Marcus Aurelius overthrew the Marcomanni, Quadi, and other German allies, the bodies of women in armor were found among the slain.

[55] Thus, in the army of Ariovistus, the women, with their hair dishevelled, and weeping, besought the soldiers not to deliver them captives to the Romans.—Cæsar, Bell. Gall. i.

[56] Relative to this, perhaps, is a circumstance mentioned by Suetonius in his Life of Augustus. "From some nations he attempted to exact a new kind of hostages, women: because he observed that those of the male sex were disregarded."—Aug. xxi.

[57] See the same observation with regard to the Celtic women, in Plutarch, on the virtues of women. The North Americans pay a similar regard to their females.

[58] A remarkable instance of this is given by Cæsar. "When he inquired of the captives the reason why Ariovistus did not engage, he learned, that it was because the matrons, who among the Germans are accustomed to pronounce, from their divinations, whether or not a battle will be favorable, had declared that they would not prove victorious, if they should fight before the new moon."—Bell. Gall. i. The cruel manner in which the Cimbrian women performed their divinations is thus related by Strabo: "The women who follow the Cimbri to war, are accompanied by gray-haired prophetesses, in white vestments, with canvas mantles fastened by clasps, a brazen girdle, and naked feet. These go with drawn swords through the camp, and, striking down those of the prisoners that they meet, drag them to a brazen kettle, holding about twenty amphorae. This has a kind of stage above it, ascending on which, the priestess cuts the throat of the victim, and, from the manner in which the blood flows into the vessel, judges of the future event. Others tear open the bodies of the captives thus butchered, and, from inspection of the entrails, presage victory to their own party."—Lib. vii.

[59] She was afterwards taken prisoner by Rutilius Gallicus. Statius, in his Sylvae, i. 4, refers to this event. Tacitus has more concerning her in his History, iv. 61.

[60] Viradesthis was a goddess of the Tungri; Harimella, another provincial deity; whose names were found by Mr. Pennant inscribed on altars at the Roman station at Burrens. These were erected by the German auxiliaries.—Vide Tour in Scotland, 1772, part ii. p. 406.

[61] Ritter considers that here is a reference to the servile flattery of the senate as exhibited in the time of Nero, by the deification of Poppaea's infant daughter, and afterwards of herself. (See Ann. xv. 23, Dion. lxiii, Ann. xiv. 3.) There is no contradiction in the present passage to that found at Hist. iv. 61, where Tacitus says, "plerasque feminarum fatidicas et, augescente superstitione, arbitrantur deas;" i.e. they deem (arbitrantur) very many of their women possessed of prophetic powers, and, as their religious feeling increases, they deem (arbitrantur) them goddesses, i.e. possessed of a superhuman nature; they do not, however, make them goddesses and worship them, as the Romans did Poppaea and her infant, which is covertly implied in facerent deas. —White.

[62] Mercury, *i.e.* a god whom Tacitus thus names, because his attributes resembled those of the Roman Mercury. According to Paulus Diaconus (de Gestis Langobardorum, i. 9), this deity was Wodun, or Gwodan, called also Odin. Mallet (North. Ant. ch. v.) says, that in the Icelandic mythology he is called "the terrible and severe God, the Father of Slaughter, he who giveth victory and receiveth courage in the conflict, who nameth those that are to be slain." "The Germans drew their gods by their own character, who loved nothing so much themselves as to display their strength and power in battle, and to signalize their vengeance upon their enemies by slaughter and desolation." There remain to this day some traces of the worship paid to Odin in the name given by almost all the people of the north to the fourth day of the week, which was formerly consecrated to him. It is called by a name which signifies "Odin's day;" "Old Norse, *Odinsdagr*; Swedish and Danish, *Onsdag*; Anglo-Saxon, *Wodenesdaeg, Wodnesdaeg*; Dutch, *Woensdag*; English, Wednesday. As Odin or Wodun was supposed to correspond to the Mercury of the Greeks and Romans, the name of this day was expressed in Latin *Dies Mercurii*."—- *White.*

[63] "The appointed time for these sacrifices," says Mallet (North. Ant. ch. vi.), "was always determined by a superstitious opinion which made the northern nations regard the number 'three' as sacred and particularly dear to the gods. Thus, in every ninth month they renewed the bloody ceremony, which was to last nine days, and every day they offered up nine living victims, whether men or animals. But the most solemn sacrifices were those which were offered up at Upsal in Sweden every ninth year...." After stating the compulsory nature of the attendance at this festival, Mallet adds, "Then they chose among the captives in time of war, and among the slaves in time of peace, nine persons to be sacrificed. In whatever manner they immolated men, the priest always took care in consecrating the victim to pronounce certain words, as 'I devote thee to Odin,' 'I send thee to Odin.'" See Lucan i. 444.

"Et quibus immitis placatur sanguine diro
Teutates, horrensque feris altaribus Hesus."

Teutates is Mercury, Hesus, Mars. So also at iii. 399, &c.

"Lucus erat longo nunquam violatus ab aevo. ... Barbara ritu Sacra Deum, structae diris altaribus arae, Omnis et humanis lustrata cruoribus arbor."

[64] That is, as in the preceding case, a deity whose attributes corresponded to those of the Roman Mars. This appears to have been not *Thor*, who is rather the representative of the Roman Jupiter, but *Tyr*, "a warrior god, and the protector of champions and brave men!" "From *Tyr* is derived the name given to the third day of the week in most of the Teutonic languages, and which has been rendered into Latin by *Dies Martis*. Old Norse, *Tirsdagr, Tisdagr*; Swedish, *Tisdag*; Danish, *Tirsdag*; German, *Dienstag*; Dutch, *Dingsdag*; Anglo-Saxon, *Tyrsdaeg, Tyvesdag, Tivesdaeg*; English, *Tuesday*"—(Mallet's North. Ant. ch. v.)—*White.*

[65] The Suevi appear to have been the Germanic tribes, and this also the worship spoken of at chap. xl. *Signum in modum liburnae figuration* corresponds with the *vehiculum* there spoken of; the real thing being, according to Ritter's view, a pinnace placed on wheels. That *signum ipsum* ("the very symbol") does not mean any image of the goddess, may be gathered also from ch. xl., where the goddess herself, *si credere velis*, is spoken of as being washed in the sacred lake.

[66] As the Romans in their ancient coins, many of which are now extant, recorded the arrival of Saturn by the stern of a ship; so other nations have frequently denoted the importation of a foreign religious rite by the figure of a galley on their medals.

[67] Tacitus elsewhere speaks of temples of German divinities (e.g. 40; Templum Nerthae, Ann. i. 51; Templum Tanfanae); but a consecrated grove, or any other sacred place, was called templum by the Romans.

[68] The Scythians are mentioned by Herodotus, and the Alans by Ammianus Marcellinus, as making use of these divining rods. The German method of divination with them is illustrated by what is said by Saxo-Grammaticus (Hist. Dan. xiv, 288) of the inhabitants of the Isle of Rugen in the Baltic Sea: "Throwing, by way of lots, three pieces of wood, white in one part, and black in another, into their laps, they foretold good fortune by the coming up of the white; bad by that of the black."

[69] The same practice obtained among the Persians, from whom the Germans appear to be sprung. Darius was elected king by the neighing of a horse; sacred white horses were in the army of Cyrus; and Xerxes, retreating after his defeat, was preceded by the sacred horses and consecrated chariot. Justin (i. 10) mentions the cause of this superstition, *viz.* that "the Persians believed the Sun to be the only God, and horses to be peculiarly consecrated to him." The priest of the Isle of Rugen also took auspices from a white horse, as may be seen in Saxo-Grammaticus.

[70] Montesquieu finds in this custom the origin of the duel, and of knight-errantry.

[71] This remarkable passage, so curious in political history, is commented on by Montesquieu, in his Spirit of Laws. vi 11. That celebrated author expresses his surprise at the existence of such a balance between liberty and authority in the forests of Germany; and traces the origin of the English constitution from this source. Tacitus again mentions the German form of government in his Annals, iv. 33.

[72] The high antiquity of this made of reckoning appears from the Book of Genesis. "The evening and the morning were the first day." The Gauls, we are informed by Cæsar, "assert that, according to the tradition of their Druids, they are all sprung from Father Dis; on which account they reckon every period of time according to the number of nights, not of days; and observe birthdays and the beginnings of months and years in such a manner, that the day seems to follow the night." (Bell. Gall. vi. 18.) The vestiges of this method of computation still appear in the English language, in the terms se'nnight and fort'night.

[73] *Ut turbae placuit.* Doederlein interprets this passage as representing the confused way in which the people took their seats in the national assembly, without reference to order, rank, age, &c. It rather represents, however, that the people, not the chieftains, determined when the business of the council should begin.—*White.*

[74] And in an open plain. Vast heaps of stone still remaining, denote the scenes of these national councils. (See Mallet's Introduct. to Hist. of Denmark.) The English Stonehenge has been supposed a relic of this kind. In these assemblies are seen the origin of those which, under the Merovingian race of French kings, were called the Fields of March; under the Carlovingian, the Fields of May; then, the Plenary Courts of Christmas and Easter; and lastly, the States General.

[75] The speech of Civilis was received with this expression of applause. Tacitus, Hist. iv. 15.

[76] Gibbeted alive. Heavy penalties were denounced against those who should take them down, alive or dead. These are particularized in the Salic law.

[77] By cowards and dastards, in this passage, are probably meant those who, being summoned to war, refused or neglected to go. Cæsar (Bell. Gall. vi. 22) mentions, that those who refused to follow their chiefs to war were considered as deserters and traitors. And, afterwards, the emperor Clothaire made the following edict, preserved in the Lombard law: "Whatever freeman, summoned to the defence of his country by his Count, or his officers, shall neglect to go, and the enemy enter the country to lay it waste, or otherwise damage our liege subjects, he shall incur a capital punishment." As the crimes of cowardice, treachery, and desertion were so odious and ignominious among the Germans, we find by the Salic law, that penalties were annexed to the unjust imputation of them.

[78] These were so rare and so infamous among the Germans, that barely calling a person by a name significant of them was severely punished.

[79] Incestuous people were buried alive in bogs in Scotland. Pennant's Tour in Scotland, 1772; part i. p. 351; and part ii. p. 421.

[80] Among these slighter offences, however, were reckoned homicide, adultery, theft, and many others of a similar kind. This appears from the laws of the Germans, and from a subsequent passage of Tacitus himself.

[81] These were at that time the only riches of the country, as was already observed in this treatise. Afterwards gold and silver became plentiful: hence all the mulcts required by the Salic law are pecuniary. Money, however, still bore a fixed proportion to cattle; as appears from the Saxon law (Tit. xviii.): "The Solidus is of two kinds; one contains two tremisses, that is, a beeve of twelve months, or a sheep with its lamb; the other, three tremisses, or a beeve of sixteen months. Homicide is compounded for by the lesser solidus; other crimes by the greater." The Saxons had

their Weregeld,—the Scotch their Cro, Galnes, and Kelchin,— and the Welsh their Gwerth, and Galanus, or compensations for injuries; and cattle were likewise the usual fine. Vide Pennant's Tour in Wales of 1773, pp. 273, 274.

[82] This mulct is frequently in the Salic law called "fred," that is, peace; because it was paid to the king or state, as guardians of the public peace.

[83] A brief account of the civil economy of the Germans will here be useful. They were divided into nations; of which some were under a regal government, others a republican. The former had kings, the latter chiefs. Both in kingdoms and republics, military affairs were under the conduct of the generals. The nations were divided into cantons; each of which was superintended by a chief, or count, who administered justice in it. The cantons were divided into districts or hundreds, so called because they contained a hundred vills or townships. In each hundred was a companion, or centenary, chosen from the people, before whom small causes were tried. Before the count, all causes, as well great as small, were amenable. The centenaries are called companions by Tacitus, after the custom of the Romans; among whom the titles of honor were, Cæsar, the Legatus or Lieutenant of Cæsar, and his comites, or companions. The courts of justice were held in the open air, on a rising ground, beneath the shade of an oak, elm, or some other large tree.

[84] Even judges were armed on the seat of justice. The Romans, on the contrary, never went armed but when actually engaged in military service.

[85] These are the rudiments of the famous institution of chivalry. The sons of kings appear to have received arms from foreign princes. Hence, when Audoin, after overcoming the Gepidae, was requested by the Lombards to dine with his son Alboin, his partner in the victory, he refused; for, says he, "you know it is not customary with us for a king's son to dine with his father, until he has received arms from the king of another country."—Warnefrid, De gestis Langobardorum, i. 23.

[86] An allusion to the *toga virilis* of the Romans. The German youth were presented with the shield and spear probably at twelve or fifteen years of age. This early initiation into the business of arms gave them that warlike character for which they were so celebrated. Thus, Seneca (Epist. 46) says, "A native of Germany brandishes, while yet a boy, his slender javelin." And again (in his book on Anger, i. 11), "Who are braver than the Germans?—who more impetuous in the charge?—who fonder of arms, in the use of which they are born and nourished, which are their only care?—who more inured to hardships, insomuch that for the most part they provide no covering for their bodies, no retreat against the perpetual severity of the climate?"

[87] Hence it seems that these noble lads were deemed *principes* in rank, yet had their position among the *comites* only. The German word *Gesell* is peculiarly appropriated to these comrades in arms. So highly were they esteemed in Germany, that for killing or hurting them a fine was exacted treble to that for other freemen.

[88] Hence, when Chonodomarus, king of the Alamanni, was taken prisoner by the Romans, "his companions, two hundred in number, and three friends peculiarly attached to him, thinking it infamous to survive their prince, or not to die for him, surrendered themselves to be put in bonds."— Ammianus Marcellinus, xvi. 13.

[89] Hence Montesquieu (Spirit of Laws, xxx, 3) justly derives the origin of vassalage. At first, the prince gave to his nobles arms and provision: as avarice advanced, money, and then lands, were required, which from benefices became at length hereditary possessions, and were called fiefs. Hence the establishment of the feudal system.

[90] Cæsar, with less precision, says, "The Germans pass their whole lives in hunting and military exercises." (Bell. Gall, vi. 21.) The picture drawn by Tacitus is more consonant to the genius of a barbarous people: besides that, hunting being the employment but of a few months of the year, a greater part must necessarily be passed in indolence by those who had no other occupation. In this circumstance, and those afterwards related, the North American savages exactly agree with the ancient Germans.

[91] This apparent contradiction is, however, perfectly agreeable to the principles of human nature. Among people governed by impulse more than reason, everything is in the extreme: war and peace; motion and rest; love and hatred; none are pursued with moderation.

[92] These are the rudiments of tributes; though the contributions here spoken of were voluntary, and without compulsion. The origin of exchequers is pointed out above, where "part of the mulct" is said to be "paid to the king or state." Taxation was taught the Germans by the Romans, who levied taxes upon them.

[93] So, in after-times, when tributes were customary, 500 oxen or cows were required annually from the Saxons by the French kings Clothaire I. and Pepin. (See Eccard, tom. i. pp. 84, 480.) Honey, corn, and other products of the earth, were likewise received in tribute. (Ibid. p. 392.)

[94] For the expenses of war, and other necessities of state, and particularly the public entertainments. Hence, besides the Steora, or annual tribute, the Osterstuopha, or Easter cup, previous to the public assembly of the Field of March, was paid to the French kings.

[95] This was a dangerous lesson, and in the end proved ruinous to the Roman empire. Herodian says of the Germans in his time, "They are chiefly to be prevailed upon by bribes; being fond of money, and continually selling peace to the Romans for gold."—Lib. vi. 139.

[96] This custom was of long duration; for there is not the mention of a single city in Ammianus Marcellinus, who wrote on the wars of the Romans in Germany. The

names of places in Ptolemy (ii. 11) are not, therefore, those of cities, but of scattered villages. The Germans had not even what we should call towns, notwithstanding Cæsar asserts the contrary.

[97] The space surrounding the house, and fenced in by hedges, was that celebrated Salic land, which descended to the male line, exclusively of the female.

[98] The danger of fire was particularly urgent in time of war; for, as Cæsar informs us, these people were acquainted with a method of throwing red-hot clay bullets from slings, and burning javelins, on the thatch of houses. (Bell. Gall. v. 42.)

[99] Thus likewise Mela (ii. 1), concerning the Sarmatians: "On account of the length and severity of their winters, they dwell under ground, either in natural or artificial caverns." At the time that Germany was laid waste by a forty years' war, Kircher saw many of the natives who, with their flocks, herds, and other possessions, took refuge in the caverns of the highest mountains. For many other curious particulars concerning these and other subterranean caves, see his Mundus Subterraneus, viii. 3, p. 100. In Hungary, at this day, corn is commonly stored in subterranean chambers.

[100] Near Newbottle, the seat of the Marquis of Lothian, are some subterraneous apartments and passages cut out of the live rock, which had probably served for the same purposes of winter-retreats and granaries as those dug by the ancient Germans. Pennant's Tour in 1769, 4to, p.63.

[101] This was a kind of mantle of a square form, called also *rheno*. Thus Cæsar (Bell. Gall. vi. 21): "They use skins for clothing, or the short rhenones, and leave the greatest part of the body naked." Isidore (xix. 23) describes the rhenones as "garments covering the shoulders and breast, as low as the navel, so rough and shaggy that they are impenetrable to rain." Mela (iii. 3), speaking of the Germans, says, "The men are clothed only with the sagum, or the bark of trees, even in the depth of winter."

[102] All savages are fond of variety of colors; hence the Germans spotted their furs with the skins of other animals, of which those here mentioned were probably of the seal kind. This practice is still continued with regard to the ermine, which is spotted with black lamb's-skin.

[103] The Northern Sea, and Frozen Ocean.

[104] Pliny testifies the same thing; and adds, that "the women beyond the Rhine are not acquainted with any more elegant kind of clothing."—xix. 1.

[105] Not that rich and costly purple in which the Roman nobility shone, but some ordinary material, such as the *vaccinium*, which Pliny says was used by the Gauls as a purple dye for the garments of the slaves, (xvi. 18.)

[106] The chastity of the Germans, and their strict regard to the laws of marriage, are witnessed by all their ancient codes of law. The purity of their manners in this respect afforded a striking contrast to the licentiousness of the Romans in the decline of the empire, and is exhibited in this light by Salvian, in his treatise De Gubernatione Dei, lib. vii.

[107] Thus we find in Cæsar (Bell. Gall. i. 53) that Ariovistus had two wives. Others had more. This indulgence proved more difficult to abolish, as it was considered as a mark of opulence, and an appendage of nobility.

[108] The Germans purchased their wives, as appears from the following clauses in the Saxon law concerning marriage: "A person who espouses a wife shall pay to her parents 300 solidi (about 180_l._ sterling); but if the marriage be without the consent of the parents, the damsel, however, consenting, he shall pay 600 solidi. If neither the parents nor damsel consent, that is, if she be carried off by violence, he shall pay 300 solidi to the parents, and 340 to the damsel, and restore her to her parents."

[109] Thus in the Saxon law, concerning dowries, it is said: "The Ostfalii and Angrarii determine, that if a woman have male issue, she is to possess the dower she received in marriage during her life, and transmit it to her sons."

[110] *Ergo septae pudiciti agunt.* Some editions have *sept pudiciti.* This would imply, however, rather the result of the care and watchfulness of their husbands; whereas it seems the object of Tacitus to show that this their chastity was the effect of innate virtue, and this is rather expressed by *septae pudiciti*, which is the reading of the Arundelian MS.

[111] Seneca speaks with great force and warmth on this subject: "Nothing is so destructive to morals as loitering at public entertainments; for vice more easily insinuates itself into the heart when softened by pleasure. What shall I say! I return from them more covetous ambitious, and luxurious."—Epist. vii.

[112] The Germans had a great regard for the hair, and looked upon cutting it off as a heavy disgrace; so that this was made a punishment for certain crimes, and was resented as an injury if practised upon an innocent person.

[113] From an epistle of St. Boniface, archbishop of Mentz, to Ethelbald, king of England, we learn that among the Saxons the women themselves inflicted the punishment for violated chastity; "In ancient Saxony (now Westphalia), if a virgin pollute her father's house, or a married woman prove false to her vows, sometimes she is forced to put an end to her own life by the halter, and over the ashes of her burned body her seducer is hanged: sometimes a troop of females assembling lead her through the circumjacent villages, lacerating her body, stripped to the girdle, with rods and knives; and thus, bloody and full of minute wounds, she is continually met by new tormenters, who in their zeal for chastity do not quit her till she is dead, or scarcely alive, in order to inspire a dread of such offences." See Michael Alford's Annales Ecclesiae Anglo-Saxon., and Eccard.

[114] A passage in Valerius Maximus renders it probable that the Cimbrian states were of this number: "The wives of the Teutones besought Marius, after his victory, that he would deliver them as a present to the Vestal virgins; affirming that they should henceforth, equally with themselves, abstain from the embraces of the other sex. This request not being granted, they all strangled themselves the ensuing night."—Lib. vi. 1.3.

[115] Among the Heruli, the wife was expected to hang herself at once at the grave of her husband, if she would not live in perpetual infamy.

[116] This expression may signify as well the murder of young children, as the procurement of abortion; both which crimes were severely punished by the German laws.

[117] *Quemquam ex agnatis.* By *agnati* generally in Roman law were meant relations by the father's side; here it signifies children born after there was already an heir to the name and property of the father.

[118] Justin has a similar thought concerning the Scythians: "Justice is cultivated by the dispositions of the people, not by the laws." (ii. 2.) How inefficacious the good laws here alluded to by Tacitus were in preventing enormities among the Romans, appears from the frequent complaints of the senators, and particularly of Minucius Felix; "I behold you, exposing your babes to the wild beasts and birds, or strangling the unhappy wretches with your own hands. Some of you, by means of drugs, extinguish the newly-formed man within your bowels, and thus commit parricide on your offspring before you bring them into the world." (Octavius, c. 30.) So familiar was this practice grown at Rome, that the virtuous Pliny apologises for it, alleging that "the great fertility of some women may require such a licence."—xxix. 4, 37.

[119] *Nudi ac sordidi* does not mean "in nakedness and filth," as most translators have supposed. Personal filth is inconsistent with the daily practice of bathing mentioned c. 22; and *nudus* does not necessarily imply absolute nakedness (see note 4, p. 293).

[120] This age appears at first to have been twelve years; for then a youth became liable to the penalties of law. Thus in the Salic law it is said, "If a child under twelve commit a fault, 'fred,' or a mulct, shall not be required of him." Afterwards the term was fifteen years of age. Thus in the Ripuary law, "A child under fifteen shall not be responsible." Again, "If a man die, or be killed, and leave a son; before he have completed his fifteenth year, he shall neither prosecute a cause, nor be called upon to answer in a suit: but at this term, he must either answer himself, or choose an advocate. In like manner with regard to the female sex." The Burgundian law provides to the same effect. This then was the term of majority, which in later times, when heavier armor was used, was still longer delayed.

[121] This is illustrated by a passage in Cæsar (Bell. Gall. vi. 21): "They who are the latest in proving their virility are most commended. By this delay they imagine

the stature is increased, the strength improved, and the nerves fortified. To have knowledge of the other sex before twenty years of age, is accounted in the highest degree scandalous."

[122] Equal not only in age and constitution, but in condition. Many of the German codes of law annex penalties to those of both sexes who marry persons of inferior rank.

[123] Hence, in the history of the Merovingian kings of France, so many instances of regard to sisters and their children appear, and so many wars undertaken on their account.

[124] The court paid at Rome to rich persons without children, by the Haeredipetae, or legacy-hunters, is a frequent subject of censure and ridicule with the Roman writers.

[125] Avengers of blood are mentioned in the law of Moses, Numb. xxxv. 19. In the Roman law also, under the head of "those who on account of unworthiness are deprived of their inheritance," it is pronounced, that "such heirs as are proved to have neglected revenging the testator's death, shall be obliged to restore the entire profits."

[126] It was a wise provision, that among this fierce and warlike people, revenge should be commuted for a payment. That this intention might not be frustrated by the poverty of the offender, his whole family were conjointly bound to make compensation.

[127] All uncivilized nations agree in this property, which becomes less necessary as a nation improves in the arts of civil life.

[128] *Convictibus et hospitiis.* "Festivities and entertainments." The former word applies to friends and fellow-countrymen; the latter, to those not of the same tribe, and foreigners. Cæsar (Bell. Gall. vi. 23) says, "They think it unlawful to offer violence to their guests, who, on whatever occasion they come to them, are protected from injury, and considered as sacred. Every house is open to them, and provision everywhere set before them." Mela (iii. 3) says of the Germans, "They make right consist in force, so that they are not ashamed of robbery: they are only kind to their guests, and merciful to suppliants. The Burgundian law lays a fine of three solidi on every man who refuses his roof or hearth to the coming guest." The Salic law, however, rightly forbids the exercise of hospitality to atrocious criminals; laying a penalty on the person who shall harbor one who has dug up or despoiled the dead? till he has made satisfaction to the relations.

[129] The clause here put within brackets is probably misplaced; since it does not connect well either with what goes before or what follows.[130] The Russians are at

present the most remarkable among the northern nations for the use of warm bathing. Some of the North American tribes also have their hypocausts, or stoves.

[131] Eating at separate tables is generally an indication of voracity. Traces of it may be found in Homer, and other writers who have described ancient manners. The same practice has also been observed among the people of Otaheite; who occasionally devour vast quantities of food.

[132] The following article in the Salic law shows at once the frequency of these bloody quarrels, and the laudable endeavors of the legislature to restrain them;—"If at a feast where there are four or five men in company, one of them be killed, the rest shall either convict one as the offender, or shall jointly pay the composition for his death. And this law shall extend to seven persons present at an entertainment."

[133] The same custom is related by Herodotus, i. p. 66, as prevailing among the Persians.

[134] Of this liquor, beer or ale, Pliny speaks in the following passage: "The western nations have their intoxicating liquor, made of steeped grain. The Egyptians also invented drinks of the same kind. Thus drunkenness is a stranger in no part of the world; for these liquors are taken pure, and not diluted as wine is. Yet, surely, the Earth thought she was producing corn. Oh, the wonderful sagacity of our vices! we have discovered how to render even water intoxicating."—xiv. 22.

[135] Mela says, "Their manner of living is so rude and savage, that they eat even raw flesh; either fresh killed, or softened by working with their hands and feet, after it has grown stiff in the hides of tame or wild animals." (iii. 3.) Florus relates that the ferocity of the Cimbri was mitigated by their feeding on bread and dressed meat, and drinking wine, in the softest tract of Italy.—iii. 3.

[136] This must not be understood to have been cheese; although Cæsar says of the Germans, "Their diet chiefly consists of milk, cheese and flesh." (Bell. Gall. vi. 22.) Pliny, who was thoroughly acquainted with the German manners, says more accurately, "It is surprising that the barbarous nations who live on milk should for so many ages have been ignorant of, or have rejected, the preparation of cheese; especially since they thicken their milk into a pleasant tart substance, and a fat butter: this is the scum of milk, of a thicker consistence than what is called the whey. It must not be omitted that it has the properties of oil, and is used as an unguent by all the barbarians, and by us for children."—xi. 41.

[137] This policy has been practised by the Europeans with regard to the North American savages, some tribes of which have been almost totally extirpated by it.

[138] St. Ambrose has a remarkable passage concerning this spirit of gaming among a barbarous people:—"It is said that the Huns, who continually make war upon other nations, are themselves subject to usurers, with whom they run in debt at play; and

that, while they live without laws, they obey the laws of the dice alone; playing when drawn up in line of battle; carrying dice along with their arms, and perishing more by each others' hands than by the enemy. In the midst of victory they submit to become captives, and suffer plunder from their own countrymen, which they know not how to bear from the foe. On this account they never lay aside the business of war, because, when they have lost all their booty by the dice, they have no means of acquiring fresh supplies for play, but by the sword. They are frequently borne away with such a desperate ardor, that, when the loser has given up his arms, the only part of his property which he greatly values, he sets the power over his life at a single cast to the winner or usurer. It is a fact, that a person, known to the Roman emperor, paid the price of a servitude which he had by this means brought upon himself, by suffering death at the command of his master."

[139] The condition of these slaves was the same as that of the vassals, or serfs, who a few centuries ago made the great body of the people in every country in Europe. The Germans, in after times, imitating the Romans, had slaves of inferior condition, to whom the name of slave became appropriated; while those in the state of rural vassalage were called *lidi*.

[140] A private enemy could not be slain with impunity, since a fine was affixed to homicide; but a man might kill his own slave without any punishment. If, however, he killed another person's slave, he was obliged to pay his price to the owner.

[141] The amazing height of power and insolence to which freedmen arrived by making themselves subservient to the vices of the prince, is a striking characteristic of the reigns of some of the worst of the Roman emperors.

[142] In Rome, on the other hand, the practice of usury was, as our author terms it, "an ancient evil, and a perpetual source of sedition and discord."—Annals, vi. 16.

[143] All the copies read *per vices*, "by turns," or alternately; but the connection seems evidently to require the easy alteration of *per vicos*, which has been approved by many learned commentators, and is therefore adopted in this translation.

[144] Cæsar has several particulars concerning this part of German polity. "They are not studious of agriculture, the greater part of their diet consisting of milk, cheese, and flesh; nor has any one a determinate portion of land, his own peculiar property; but the magistrates and chiefs allot every year to tribes and clanships forming communities, as much land, and in such situations, as they think proper, and oblige them to remove the succeeding year. For this practice they assign several reasons: as, lest they should be led, by being accustomed to one spot, to exchange the toils of war for the business of agriculture; lest they should acquire a passion for possessing extensive domains, and the more powerful should be tempted to dispossess the weaker; lest they should construct buildings with more art than was necessary to protect them from the inclemencies of the weather; lest the love of money should arise amongst them, the source of faction and dissensions; and in order that the

people, beholding their own possessions equal to those of the most powerful, might be retained by the bonds of equity and moderation."—Bell. Gall. vi. 21.

[145] The Germans, not planting fruit-trees, were ignorant of the proper products of autumn. They have now all the autumnal fruits of their climate; yet their language still retains a memorial of their ancient deficiencies, in having no term for this season of the year, but one denoting the gathering in of corn alone—*Herbst*, Harvest.

[146] In this respect, as well as many others, the manners of the Germans were a direct contrast to those of the Romans. Pliny mentions a private person, C. Caecilius Claudius Isidorus, who ordered the sum of about 10,000_l._ sterling to be expended in his funeral: and in another place he says, "Intelligent persons asserted that Arabia did not produce such a quantity of spices in a year as Nero burned at the obsequies of his Poppaea."—xxxiii. 10, and xii. 18.

[147] The following lines of Lucan, describing the last honors paid by Cornelia to the body of Pompey the Great, happily illustrate the customs here referred to:—

Collegit vestes, miserique insignia Magni.
Armaque, et impressas auro, quas gesserat olim
Exuvias, pictasque togas, velamina summo
Ter conspecta Jovi, funestoque intulit igni.—Lib. ix. 175.

"There shone his arms, with antique gold inlaid,
There the rich robes which she herself had made,
Robes to imperial Jove in triumph thrice display'd:
The relics of his past victorious days,
Now this his latest trophy serve to raise,
And in one common flame together blaze."—ROWE.

[148] Thus in the tomb of Childeric, king of the Franks, were found his spear and sword, and also his horse's head, with a shoe, and gold buckles and housings. A human skull was likewise discovered, which, perhaps, was that of his groom.

[149] Caesar's account is as follows:—"There was formerly a time when the Gauls surpassed the Germans in bravery, and made war upon them; and, on account of their multitude of people and scarcity of land, sent colonies beyond the Rhine. The most fertile parts of Germany, adjoining to the Hercynian forest, (which, I observe, was known by report to Eratosthenes and others of the Greeks, and called by them Orcinia,) were accordingly occupied by the Volcae and Tectosages, who settled there. These people still continue in the same settlements, and have a high character as well for the administration of justice as military prowess: and they now remain in the same state of penury and content as the Germans, whose manner of life they have adopted."—Bell. Gall. vi. 24.

[150] The inhabitants of Switzerland, then extending further than at present, towards Lyons.

[151] A nation of Gauls, bordering on the Helvetii, as appears from Strabo and Cæsar. After being conquered by Cæsar, the Aedui gave them a settlement in the country now called the Bourbonnois. The name of their German colony, Boiemum, is still extant in Bohemia. The aera at which the Helvetii and Boii penetrated into Germany is not ascertained. It seems probable, however, that it was in the reign of Tarquinius Priscus; for at that time, as we are told by Livy, Ambigatus, king of the Bituriges (people of Berry), sent his sister's son Sigovesus into the Hercynian forest, with a colony, in order to exonerate his kingdom which was overpeopled. (Livy, v. 33; *et seq.*)

[152] In the time of Augustus, the Boii, driven from Boiemum by the Marcomanni, retired to Noricum, which from them was called Boioaria, now Bavaria.

[153] This people inhabited that part of Lower Hungary now called the Palatinate of Pilis.

[154] Towards the end of this treatise, Tacitus seems himself to decide this point, observing that their use of the Pannonian language, and acquiescence in paying tribute, prove the Osi not to be a German nation. They were settled beyond the Marcomanni and Quadi, and occupied the northern part of Transdanubian Hungary; perhaps extending to Silesia, where is a place called Ossen in the duchy of Oels, famous for salt and glass works. The learned Pelloutier, however, contends that the Osi were Germans; but with less probability.

[155] The inhabitants of the modern diocese of Treves.

[156] Those of Cambresis and Hainault.

[157] Those of the dioceses of Worms, Strasburg, and Spires.

[158] Those of the diocese of Cologne. The Ubii, migrating from Germany to Gaul, on account of the enmity of the Catti, and their own attachment to the Roman interest, were received under the protection of Marcus Agrippa, in the year of Rome 717. (Strabo, iv. p. 194.) Agrippina, the wife of Claudius and mother of Nero, who was born among them, obtained the settlement of a colony there, which was called after her name.

[159] Now the Betuwe, part of the provinces of Holland and Guelderland.

[160] Hence the Batavi are termed, in an ancient inscription, "the brothers and friends of the Roman people."

[161] This nation inhabited part of the countries now called the Weteraw, Hesse, Isenburg and Fulda. In this territory was Mattium, now Marpurg, and the Fontes Mattiaci, now Wisbaden, near Mentz.

[162] The several people of Germany had their respective borders, called marks or marches, which they defended by preserving them in a desert and uncultivated state. Thus Cæsar, Bell. Gall. iv 3:—"They think it the greatest honor to a nation, to have as wide an extent of vacant land around their dominions as possible; by which it is indicated, that a great number of neighboring communities are unable to withstand them. On this account, the Suevi are said to have, on one side, a tract of 600 (some learned men think we should read 60) miles desert for their boundaries." In another place Cæsar mentions, as an additional reason for this policy, that they think themselves thereby rendered secure from the danger of sudden incursions. (Bell. Gall. vi. 13.)

[163] The difference between the low situation and moist air of Batavia, and the high and dry country of the Mattiaci, will sufficiently justify this remark, in the opinion of those who allow anything to the influence of climate.

[164] Now Swabia. When the Marcommanni, towards the end of the reign of Augustus, quitting their settlements near the Rhine, migrated to Bohemia, the lands they left vacant were occupied by some unsettled Gauls among the Rauraci and Sequani. They seem to have been called Decumates (Decimated), because the inhabitants, liable to the incursions of the Germans, paid a tithe of their products to be received under the protection of the Romans. Adrian defended them by a rampart, which extended from Neustadt, a town on the Danube near the mouth of the river Altmhl, to the Neckar near Wimpfen; a space of sixty French leagues.

[165] Of Upper Germany.

[166] The Catti possessed a large territory between the Rhine, Mayne and Sala, and the Hartz forest on this side of the Weser; where are now the countries of Hesse, Thuringia, part of Paderborn, of Fulda, and of Franconia. Learned writers have frequently noted, that what Cæsar, Florus and Ptolemy have said of the Suevi, is to be understood of the Catti. Leibnitz supposes the Catti were so called from the active animal which they resemble in name, the German for cat being *Catte*, or *Hessen*.

[167] Pliny, who was well acquainted with Germany, gives a very striking description of the Hercynian forest:—"The vast trees of the Hercynian forest, untouched for ages, and as old as the world, by their almost immortal destiny exceed common wonders. Not to mention circumstances which would not be credited, it is certain that hills are raised by the repercussion of their meeting roots; and where the earth does not follow them, arches are formed as high as the branches, which, struggling, as it were, with each other, are bent into the form of open gates, so wide, that troops of horse may ride under them."—xvi. 2.

[168] *Duriora corpora.* "Hardier frames;" *i.e.* than the rest of the Germans. At Hist. ii 32. the Germans, in general, are said to have *fluxa corpora*; while in c. 4 of this treatise they are described as *tantm ad impetum valida.*

[169] Floras, ii. 18, well expresses this thought by the sentence "Tanti exercitus, quanti imperator." "An army is worth so much as its general is."

[170] Thus Civilis is said by our author (Hist. iv. 61), to have let his hair and beard grow in consequence of a private vow. Thus too, in Paul Warnefrid's "History of the Lombards," iii. 7, it is related, that "six thousand Saxons who survived the war, vowed that they would never cut their hair, nor shave their beards, till they had been revenged of their enemies, the Suevi." A later instance of this custom is mentioned by Strada (Bell. Belg. vii. p. 344), of William Lume, one of the Counts of Mark, "who bound himself by a vow not to cut his hair till he had revenged the deaths of Egmont and Horn."

[171] The iron ring seems to have been a badge of slavery. This custom was revived in later times, but rather with a gallant than a military intention. Thus, in the year 1414, John duke of Bourbon, in order to ingratiate himself with his mistress, vowed, together with sixteen knights and gentlemen, that they would wear, he and the knights a gold ring, the gentlemen a silver one, round their left legs, every Sunday for two years, till they had met with an equal number of knights and gentlemen to contend with them in a tournament. (Vertot, Mm. de l'Acad. des Inscr. tom. ii. p. 596.)

[172] It was this nation of Catti, which, about 150 years afterwards, uniting with the remains of the Cherusci on this side the Weser, the Attuarii, Sicambri, Chamavi, Bructeri, and Chauci, entered into the Francic league, and, conquering the Romans, seized upon Gaul. From them are derived the name, manners, and laws of the French.

[173] These two tribes, united by a community of wars and misfortunes, had formerly been driven from the settlements on the Rhine a little below Mentz. They then, according to Cæsar (Bell. Gall. iv. 1, *et seq.*), occupied the territories of the Menapii on both sides the Rhine. Still proving unfortunate, they obtained the lands of the Sicambri, who, in the reign of Augustus, were removed on this side the Rhine by Tiberius: these were the present counties of Berg, Mark, Lippe, and Waldeck; and the bishopric of Paderborn.

[174] Their settlements were between the rivers Rhine, Lippe (Luppia), and Ems (Amisia), and the province of Friesland; now the countries of Westphalia and Over-Issel. Alting (Notit. German. Infer, p. 20) supposes they derived their name from *Broeken*, or *Bruchen*, marshes, on account of their frequency in that tract of country.

[175] Before this migration, the Chamavi were settled on the Ems, where at present are Lingen and Osnaburg; the Angrivarii, on the Weser (Visurgis), where are Minden and Schawenburg. A more ancient migration of the Chamavi to the banks of the

Rhine is cursorily mentioned by Tacitus, Annal. xiii. 55. The Angrivarii were afterwards called Angrarii, and became part of the Saxon nation.

[176] They were not so entirely extirpated that no relics of them remained. They were even a conspicuous part of the Francic league, as before related. Claudian also, in his panegyric on the fourth consulate of Honorius, v. 450, mentions them.

> Venit accola sylvae
> Bructerus Hercyniae.

"The Bructerian, borderer on the Hercynian forest, came."

After their expulsion, they settled, according to Eccard, between Cologne and Hesse.

[177] The Bructeri were under regal government, and maintained many wars against the Romans. Hence their arrogance and power. Before they were destroyed by their countrymen, Vestricius Spurinna terrified them into submission without an action, and had on that account a triumphal statue decreed him. Pliny the younger mentions this fact, book ii. epist. 7.

[178] An allusion to gladiatorial spectacles. This slaughter happened near the canal of Drusus, where the Roman guard on the Rhine could be spectators of the battle. The account of it came to Rome in the first year of Trajan.

[179] As this treatise was written in the reign of Trajan, when the affairs of the Romans appeared unusually prosperous, some critics have imagined that Tacitus wrote *vigentibus*, "flourishing," instead of *urgentibus*, "urgent." But it is sufficiently evident, from other passages, that the causes which were operating gradually, but surely, to the destruction of the Roman empire, did not escape the penetration of Tacitus, even when disguised by the most flattering appearances. The common reading is therefore, probably, right.—*Aikin.*

[180] These people first resided near the head of the Lippe; and then removed to the settlements of the Chamavi and Angrivarii, who had expelled the Bructeri. They appear to have been the same with those whom Velleius Paterculus, ii. 105, calls the Attuarii, and by that name they entered into the Francic league. Strabo calls them Chattuarii.

[181] Namely, the Ansibarii and Tubantes. The Ansibarii or Amsibarii are thought by Alting to have derived their name from their neighborhood to the river Ems (Amisia); and the. Tubantes, from their frequent change of habitation, to have been called *Tho Benten.* or the wandering troops, and to have dwelt where now is Drente in Over-Issel. Among these nations, Furstenburg (Monum. Paderborn.) enumerates the Ambrones, borderers upon the river Ambrus, now Emmeren.

[182] The Frieslanders. The lesser Frisii were settled on this side, the greater, on the other, of the Flevum (Zuyderzee).

[183] In the time of the Romans this country was covered by vast meres, or lakes; which were made still larger by frequent inundations of the sea. Of these, one so late as 1530 overwhelmed seventy-two villages; and another, still more terrible, in 1569, laid under water great part of the sea-coast of Holland, and almost all Friesland, in which alone 20,000 persons were drowned.

[184] Wherever the land seemed to terminate, and it appeared impossible to proceed further, maritime nations have feigned pillars of Hercules. Those celebrated by the Frisians must have been at the extremity of Friesland, and not in Sweden and the Cimmerian promontory, as Rudbeck supposes.

[185] Drusus, the brother of Tiberius, and father of Germanicus, imposed a tribute on the Frisians, as mentioned in the Annals, iv. 72, and performed other eminent services in Germany; himself styled Germanicus.

[186] The Chauci extended along the seacoast from the Ems to the Elbe (Albis); whence they bordered on all the fore-mentioned nations, between which and the Cherusci they came round to the Catti. The Chauci were distinguished into Greater and Lesser. The Greater, according to Ptolemy, inhabited the country between the Weser and the Elbe; the Lesser, that between the Weser and Ems; but Tacitus (Annals xi. 19) seems to reverse this order. Alting supposes the Chauci had their name from *Kauken*, signifying persons eminent for valor and fidelity, which agrees with the character Tacitus gives them. Others derive it from *Kauk*, an owl, with a reference to the enmity of that animal to cats (*Catti*). Others, from *Kaiten*, daws, of which there are great numbers on their coast. Pliny has admirably described the country and manners of the maritime Chauci, in his account of people who live without any trees or fruit-bearing vegetables: —"In the North are the nations of Chauci, who are divided into Greater and Lesser. Here, the ocean, having a prodigious flux and reflux twice in the space of every day and night, rolls over an immense tract, leaving it a matter of perpetual doubt whether it is part of the land or sea. In this spot, the wretched natives, occupying either the tops of hills, or artificial mounds of turf, raised out of reach of the highest tides, build their small cottages; which appear like sailing vessels when the water covers the circumjacent ground, and like wrecks when it has retired. Here from their huts they pursue the fish, continually flying from them with the waves. They do not, like their neighbors, possess cattle, and feed on milk; nor have they a warfare to maintain against wild beasts, for every fruit of the earth is far removed from them. With flags and seaweed they twist cordage for their fishing-nets. For fuel they use a kind of mud, taken up by hand, and dried, rather in the wind than the sun: with this earth they heat their food, and warm their bodies, stiffened by the rigorous north. Their only drink is rain-water collected in ditches at the thresholds of their doors. Yet this miserable people, if conquered to-day by the Roman arms, would call themselves slaves. Thus it is that fortune spares many to their own punishment."—Hist. Nat. xvi. 1.

70

[187] On this account, fortified posts were established by the Romans to restrain the Chauci; who by Lucan are called Cayci in the following passage:

Et vos crinigeros bellis arcere Caycos
Oppositi.—Phars. i. 463.

"You, too, tow'rds Rome advance, ye warlike band,
That wont the shaggy Cauci to withstand."—ROWE

[188] The Cherusci, at that time, dwelt between the Weser and the Elbe, where now are Luneburg, Brunswick, and part of the Marche of Brandenburg on this side the Elbe. In the reign of Augustus they occupied a more extensive tract; reaching even this side the Weser, as appears from the accounts of the expedition of Drusus given by Dio and Velleius Paterculus: unless, as Dithmar observes, what is said of the Cherusci on this side the Weser relates to the Dulgibini, their dependents. For, according to Strabo, Varus was cut off by the Cherusci, and the people subject to them. The brave actions of Arminius, the celebrated chief of the Cherusci, are related by Tacitus in the 1st and 2d books of his Annals.

[189] Cluver, and several others, suppose the Fosi to have been the same with the ancient Saxons: but, since they bordered on the Cherusci, the opinion of Leibnitz is nearer the truth, that they inhabited the banks of the river Fusa, which enters the Aller (Allera) at Cellae; and were a sort of appendage to the Cherusci, as Hildesheim now is to Brunswick. The name of Saxons is later than Tacitus, and was not known till the reign of Antoninus Pius, at which period they poured forth from the Cimbric Chersonesus, and afterwards, in conjunction with the Angles, seized upon Britain.

[191] The name of this people still exists; and the country they inhabited is called the Cimbric Chersonesus, or Peninsula; comprehending Jutland, Sleswig, and Holstein. The renown and various fortune of the Cimbri is briefly, but accurately, related by Mallet in the "Introduction" to the "History of Denmark."

[192] Though at this time they were greatly reduced by migrations, inundations and wars, they afterwards revived; and from this storehouse of nations came forth the Franks, Saxons, Normans, and various other tribes, which brought all Europe under Germanic sway.

[193] Their fame spread through Germany, Gaul, Spain, Britain, Italy, and as far as the Sea of Azoph (Palus Maeotis), whither, according to Posidonius, they penetrated, and called the Cimmerian or Cimbrian Bosphorus after their own name.

[194] This is usually, and probably rightly, explained as relating to both shores of the Cimbric Chersonesus. Cluver and Dithmar, however, suppose that these encampments are to be sought for either in Italy, upon the river Athesis (Adige), or in Narbonnensian Gaul near Aquae Sextiae (Aix in Provence), where Florus (iii. 3) mentions that the Teutoni defeated by Marius took post in a valley with a river

71

running through it. Of the prodigious numbers of the Cimbri who made this terrible irruption we have an account in Plutarch, who relates that their fighting men were 300,000, with a much greater number of women and children. (Plut. Marius, p. 411.)

[195] Nerva was consul the fourth time, and Trajan the second, in the 851st year of Rome; in which Tacitus composed this treatise.

[196] After the defeat of P. Decidius Saxa, lieutenant of Syria, by the Parthians, and the seizure of Syria by Pacorus, son of king Orodes, P. Ventidius Bassus was sent there, and vanquished the Parthians, killed Pacorus, and entirely restored the Roman affairs.

[197] The Epitome of Livy informs us, that "in the year of Rome 640, the Cimbri, a wandering tribe, made a predatory incursion into Illyricum, where they routed the consul Papirius Carbo with his army." According to Strabo, it was at Noreia, a town of the Taurisci, near Aquileia, that Carbo was defeated. In the succeeding years, the Cimbri and Teutonia ravaged Gaul, and brought great calamities on that country; but at length, deterred by the unshaken bravery of the Gauls, they turned another way; as appears from Cæsar, Bell. Gal. vii. 17. They then came into Italy, and sent ambassadors to the Senate, demanding lands to settle on. This was refused; and the consul M. Junius Silanus fought an unsuccessful battle with them, in the year of Rome 645. (Epitome of Livy, lxv.)

[198] "L. Cassius the consul, in the year of Rome 647, was cut off with his army in the confines of the Allobroges, by the Tigurine Gauls, a canton of the Helvetians (now the cantons of Zurich, Appenzell, Schaffhausen, &c.), who had migrated from their settlements. The soldiers who survived the slaughter gave hostages for the payment of half they were worth, to be dismissed with safety." (Ibid.) Cæsar further relates that the Roman army was passed under the yoke by the Tigurini:—"This single canton, migrating from home, within the memory of our fathers, slew the consul L. Cassius, and passed his army under the yoke."—Bell. Gall. i. 12.

[199] M. Aurelius Scaurus, the consul's lieutenant (or rather consul, as he appears to have served that office in the year of Rome 646), was defeated and taken by the Cimbri; and when, being asked his advice, he dissuaded them from passing the Alps into Italy, assuring them the Romans were invincible, he was slain by a furious youth, named Boiorix. (Epit. Livy, lxvii.)

[200] Florus, in like manner, considers these two affairs separately:— "Neither could Silanus sustain the first onset of the barbarians; nor Manlius, the second; nor Caepio, the third." (iii. 3.) Livy joins them together:—"By the same enemy (the Cimbri) Cn. Manlius the consul, and Q. Servilius Caepio the proconsul, were defeated in an engagement, and both dispossessed of their camps." (Epit. lxvii.) Paulus Orosius relates the affair more particularly:—"Manlius the consul, and Q. Caepio, proconsul, being sent against the Cimbri, Teutones, Tigurini, and Ambronae, Gaulish and German nations, who had conspired to extinguish the Roman empire, divided their respective provinces by the river Rhone. Here, the most violent dissensions

prevailing between them, they were both overcome, to the great disgrace and danger of the Roman name. According to Antias, 80,000 Romans and allies were slaughtered. Caepio, by whose rashness this misfortune was occasioned, was condemned, and his property confiscated by order of the Roman people." (Lib. v. 16.) This happened in the year of Rome 649; and the anniversary was reckoned among the unlucky days.

[201] The Republic; in opposition to Rome when governed by emperors.

[202] This tragical catastrophe so deeply affected Augustus, that, as Seutonius informs us, "he was said to have let his beard and hair grow for several months; during which he at times struck his head against the doors, crying out, 'Varus, restore my legions!' and ever after kept the anniversary as a day of mourning." (Aug. s. 23.) The finest history piece, perhaps, ever drawn by a writer, is Tacitus's description of the army of Germanicus visiting the field of battle, six years after, and performing funeral obsequies to the scattered remains of their slaughtered countrymen. (Annals, i. 61.)

[203] "After so many misfortunes, the Roman people thought no general so capable of repelling such formidable enemies, as Marius." Nor was the public opinion falsified. In his fourth consulate, in the year of Rome 652. "Marius engaged the Teutoni beyond the Alps near Aquae Sextiae (Aix in Province), killing, on the day of battle and the following day, above 150,000 of the enemy, and entirely cutting off the Teutonic nation." (Velleus Paterculus, ii. 12.) Livy says there were 200,000 slain, and 90,000 taken prisoners. The succeeding year he defeated the Cimbri, who had penetrated into Italy and crossed the Adige, in the Raudian plain, where now is Rubio, killing and taking prisoners upwards of 100,000 men. That he did not, however, obtain an unbought victory over this warlike people, may be conjectured from the resistance he met with even from their women. We are told by Florus (iii. 3) that "he was obliged to sustain an engagement with their wives, as well as themselves; who, entrenching themselves on all sides with wagons and cars, fought from them, as from towers, with lances and poles. Their death was no less glorious than their resistance. For, when they could not obtain from Marius what they requested by an embassy, their liberty, and admission into the vestal priesthood (which, indeed, could not lawfully be granted); after strangling their infants, they either fell by mutual wounds, or hung themselves on trees or the poles of their carriages in ropes made of their own hair. King Boiorix was slain, not unrevenged, fighting bravely in the field." On account of these great victories, Marius, in the year of Borne 652, triumphed over the Teutoni, Ambroni, and Cimbri.

[204] In the 596th year of Rome, Julius Cæsar defeated Ariovistus, a German king, near Dampierre in the Franche-Comte, and pursued his routed troops with great slaughter thirty miles towards the Rhine, filling all that space with spoils and dead bodies. (Bell. Gall. i. 33 and 52.) He had before chastised the Tigurini, who, as already mentioned, had defeated and killed L. Cassius. Drusus: This was the son of Livia, and brother of the emperor Tiberius. He was in Germany B.C. 12, 11. His loss was principally from shipwreck on the coast of the Chauci. See Lynam's

Roman Emperors, i. 37, 45, Nero; *i.e.* Tiberius, afterwards emperor. His name was Tiberius Claudius Drusus Nero. See Lynam's Roman Emperors, i. 51, 53, 62, 78. Germanicus: He was the son of Drusus, and so nephew of Tiberius. His victories in Germany took place A.D. 14-16. He too, like his father, was shipwrecked, and nearly at the same spot. See Lynam's Roman Emperors, i. 103-118.

[205] In the war of Civilis, related by Tacitus, Hist. iv. and v.

[206] By Domitian, as is more particularly mentioned in the Life of Agricola.

[207] The Suevi possessed that extensive tract of country lying between the Elbe, the Vistula, the Baltic Sea, and the Danube. They formerly had spread still further, reaching even to the Rhine. Hence Strabo, Cæsar, Florus, and others, have referred to the Suevi what related to the Catti.

[208] Among the Suevi, and also the rest of the Germans, the slaves, seem to have been shaven; or at least cropped so short that they could not twist or tie up their hair in a knot.

[209] The Semnones inhabited both banks of the Viadrus (Oder); the country which is now part of Pomerania, of the Marche of Brandenburg, and of Lusatia.

[210] In the reign of Augustus, the Langobardi dwelt on this side the Elbe, between Luneburg and Magdeburg. When conquered and driven beyond the Elbe by Tiberius, they occupied that part of the country where are now Prignitz, Ruppin, and part of the Middle Marche. They afterwards founded the Lombard kingdom in Italy; which, in the year of Christ 774, was destroyed by Charlemagne, who took their king Desiderius, and subdued all Italy. The laws of the Langobardi are still extant, and may be met with in Lindenbrog. The Burgundians are not mentioned by Tacitus, probably because they were then an inconsiderable people. Afterwards, joining with the Langobardi, they settled on the Decuman lands and the Roman boundary. They from thence made an irruption into Gaul, and seized that country which is still named from them Burgundy. Their laws are likewise extant.

[211] From Tacitus's description, the Reudigni must have dwelt in part of the present duchy of Mecklenburg, and of Lauenburg. They had formerly been settled on this side the Elbe, on the sands of Luneburg.

[212] Perhaps the same people with those called by Mamertinus, in his Panegyric on Maximian, the Chaibones. From their vicinity to the fore-mentioned nations, they must have inhabited part of the duchy of Mecklenburg. They had formerly dwelt on this side the Elbe, on the banks of the river Ilmenavia in Luneburg; which is now called Ava; whence, probably, the name of the people.

[213] Inhabitants of what is now part of Holstein and Sleswig; in which tract is still a district called Angeln, between Flensborg and Sleswig. In the fifth century, the

Angles, in conjunction with the Saxons, migrated into Britain, and perpetuated their name by giving appellation to England.

[214] From the enumeration of Tacitus, and the situation of the other tribes, it appears that the Eudoses must have occupied the modern Wismar and Rostock; the Suardones, Stralsund, Swedish Pomerania, and part of the Hither Pomerania, and of the Uckerane Marche. Eccard, however, supposes these nations were much more widely extended; and that the Eudoses dwelt upon the Oder; the Suardones, upon the Warte; the Nuithones, upon the Netze.

[215] The ancient name of the goddess Herth still subsists in the German *Erde*, and in the English *Earth*.

[216] Many suppose this island to have been the isle of Rugen in the Baltic sea. It is more probable, however, that it was an island near the mouth of the Elbe, now called the isle of Helgeland, or Heiligeland (Holy Island). Besides the proof arising from the name, the situation agrees better with that of the nations before enumerated.

[217] Olaus Rudbeck contends that this festival was celebrated in winter, and still continues in Scandinavia under the appellation of Julifred, the peace of Juul. (Yule is the term used for Christmas season in the old English and Scottish dialects.) But this feast was solemnized not in honor of the Earth, but of the Sun, called by them Thor or Taranium. The festival of Herth was held later, in the month of February; as may be seen in Mallet's "Introduction to the History of Denmark."

[218] *Templo* here means merely "the consecrated place," *i.e.* the grove before mentioned, for according to c.9 the Germans built no temples.

[219] It is supposed that this people, on account of their valor, were called Heermanner; corrupted by the Romans into Hermunduri. They were first settled between the Elbe, the Sala, and Bohemia; where now are Anhalt, Voightland, Saxony, part of Misnia, and of Franconia. Afterwards, when the Marcomanni took possession of Bohemia, from which the Boii had been expelled by Maroboduus, the Hermunduri added their settlements to their own, and planted in them the Suevian name, whence is derived the modern appellation of that country, Suabia.

[220] They were so at that time; but afterwards joined with the Marcomanni and other Germans against the Romans in the time of Marcus Aurelius, who overcame them.

[221] Augusta Vindelicorum, now Augsburg; a famous Roman colony in the province of Rhaetia, of which Vindelica was then a part.

[222] Tacitus is greatly mistaken if he confounds the source of the Egra, which is in the country of the Hermuduri, with that of the Elbe, which rises in Bohemia. The Elbe had been formerly, as Tacitus observes, well known to the Romans by the

victories of Drusus, Tiberius, and Domitius; but afterwards, when the increasing power of the Germans kept the Roman arms at a distance, it was only indistinctly heard of. Hence its source was probably inaccurately laid down in the Roman geographical tables. Perhaps, however, the Hermunduri, when they had served in the army of Maroboduus, received lands in that part of Bohemia in which the Elbe rises; in which case there would be no mistake in Tacitus's account.

[223] Inhabitants of that part of Bavaria which lies between Bohemia and the Danube.

[224] Inhabitants of Bohemia.

[225] Inhabitants of Moravia, and the part of Austria between it and the Danube. Of this people, Ammianus Marcellinus, in his account of the reign of Valentinian and Valens, thus speaks:—"A sudden commotion arose among the Quadi; a nation at present of little consequence, but which was formerly extremely warlike and potent, as their exploits sufficiently evince."—xxix. 15.

[226] Their expulsion of the Boii, who had given name to Bohemia, has been already mentioned. Before this period, the Marcomanni dwelt near the sources of the Danube, where now is the duchy of Wirtemburg; and, as Dithmar supposes, on account of their inhabiting the borders of Germany, were called Marcmanner, from *Marc* (the same with the old English *March*) a border, or boundary.

[227] These people justified their military reputation by the dangerous war which, in conjunction with the Marcomanni, they excited against the Romans, in the reign of Marcus Aurelius.

[228] Of this prince, and his alliance with the Romans against Arminius, mention is made by Tacitus, Annals, ii.

[229] Thus Vannius was made king of the Quadi by Tiberius. (See Annals, ii. 63.) At a later period, Antoninus Pius (as appears from a medal preserved in Spanheim) gave them Furtius for their king. And when they had expelled him, and set Ariogaesus on the throne, Marcus Aurelius, to whom he was obnoxious, refused to confirm the election. (Dio, lxxi.)

[230] These people inhabited what is now Galatz, Jagerndorf, and part of Silesia.

[231] Inhabitants of part of Silesia, and of Hungary.

[232] Inhabitants of part of Hungary to the Danube.

[233] These were settled about the Carpathian mountains, and the sources of the Vistula.

[234] It is probable that the Suevi were distinguished from the rest of the Germans by a peculiar dialect, as well as by their dress and manners.

[235] Ptolemy mentions iron mines in or near the country of the Quadi. I should imagine that the expression "additional disgrace" (or, more literally, "which might make them more ashamed") does not refer merely to the slavery of working in mines, but to the circumstance of their digging up iron, the substance by means of which they might acquire freedom and independence. This is quite in the manner of Tacitus. The word *iron* was figuratively used by the ancients to signify military force in general. Thus Solon, in his well-known answer to Croesus, observed to him, that the nation which possessed more iron would be master of all his gold.— *Aikin*.

[236] The mountains between Moravia, Hungary, Silesia, and Bohemia.

[237] The Lygii inhabited what is now part of Silesia, of the New Marche, of Prussia and Poland on this side the Vistula.

[238] These tribes were settled between the Oder and Vistula, where now are part of Silesia, of Brandenburg, and of Poland. The Elysii are supposed to have given name to Silesia.

[239] The Greeks and Romans, under the name of the Dioscuri, or Castor and Pollux, worshipped those meteorous exhalations which, during a storm, appear on the masts of ships, and are supposed to denote an approaching calm. A kind of religious veneration is still paid to this phenomenon by the Roman Catholics, under the appellation of the fire of St. Elmo. The Naharvali seem to have affixed the same character of divinity on the *ignis fatuus*; and the name Alcis is probably the same with that of Alff or Alp, which the northern nations still apply to the fancied Genii of the mountains. The Sarmatian deities Lebus and Polebus, the memory of whom still subsists in the Polish festivals, had, perhaps, the same origin.

[240] No custom has been more universal among uncivilized people than painting the body, either for the purpose of ornament, or that of inspiring terror.

[241] Inhabitants of what is now Further Pomerania, the New Marche and the Western part of Poland, between the Oder and Vistula. They were a different people from the Goths, though, perhaps, in alliance with them.

[242] These people were settled on the shore of the Baltic, where now are Colburg, Cassubia, and Further Pomerania. Their name is still preserved in the town of Rugenwald and Isle of Rugen.

[243] These were also settlers on the Baltic, about the modern Stolpe, Dantzig, and Lauenburg. The Heruli appear afterwards to have occupied the settlements of the Lemovii. Of these last no further mention occurs; but the Heruli made themselves

famous throughout Europe and Asia, and were the first of the Germans who founded a kingdom in Italy under Odoacer.

[244] The Suiones inhabited Sweden, and the Danish isles of Funen, Langlaud, Zeeland, Laland, &c. From them and the Cimbri were derived the Normans, who, after spreading terror through various parts of the empire, at last seized upon the fertile province of Normandy in France. The names of Goths, Visigoths, and Ostrogoths, became still more famous, they being the nations who accomplished the ruin of the Roman empire. The laws of the Visigoths are still extant; but they depart much from the usual simplicity of the German laws.

[245] The Romans, who had but an imperfect knowledge of this part of the world, imagined here those "vast insular tracts" mentioned in the beginning of this treatise. Hence Pliny, also, says of the Baltic sea (Codanus sinus), that "it is filled with islands, the most famous of which, Scandinavia (now Sweden and Norway), is of an undiscovered magnitude; that part of it only being known which is occupied by the Hilleviones, a nation inhabiting five hundred cantons; who call this country another globe." (Lib. iv. 13.) The memory of the Hilleviones is still preserved in the part of Sweden named Halland.

[246] Their naval power continued so great, that they had the glory of framing the nautical code, the laws of which were first written at Wisby, the capital of the isle of Gothland, in the eleventh century.

[247] This is exactly the form of the Indian canoes, which, however, are generally worked with sails as well as oars.

[248] The great opulence of a temple of the Suiones, as described by Adam of Bremen (Eccl. Hist. ch. 233), is a proof of the wealth that at all times has attended naval dominion. "This nation," says he, "possesses a temple of great renown, called Ubsola (now Upsal), not far from the cities Sictona and Birca (now Sigtuna and Bioerkoe). In this temple, which is entirely ornamented with gold, the people worship the statues of three gods; the most powerful of whom, Thor, is seated on a couch in the middle; with Woden on one side, and Fricca on the other." From the ruins of the towns Sictona and Birca arose the present capital of Sweden, Stockholm.

[249] Hence Spener (Notit. German. Antiq.) rightly concludes that the crown was hereditary, and not elective, among the Suiones.

[250] It is uncertain whether what is now called the Frozen Ocean is here meant, or the northern extremities of the Baltic Sea, the Gulfs of Bothnia and Finland, which are so frozen every winter as to be unnavigable.

[251] The true principles of astronomy have now taught us the reason why, at a certain latitude, the sun, at the summer solstice, appears never to set: and at a lower latitude, the evening twilight continues till morning.

[252] The true reading here is, probably, "immerging;" since it was a common notion at that period, that the descent of the sun into the ocean was attended with a kind of hissing noise, like red hot iron dipped into water. Thus Juvenal, Sat. xiv, 280:—

Audiet Herculeo stridentem gurgite solem.
"Hear the sun hiss in the Herculean gulf."

[253] Instead of formas deorum, "forms of deities," some, with more probability, read equorum, "of the horses," which are feigned to draw the chariot of the sun.

[254] Thus Quintus Curtius, speaking of the Indian Ocean, says, "Nature itself can proceed no further."

[255] The Baltic Sea.

[256] Now, the kingdom of Prussia, the duchies of Samogitia and Courland, the palatinates of Livonia and Esthonia, in the name of which last the ancient appellation of these people is preserved.

[257] Because the inhabitants of this extreme part of Germany retained the Scythico-Celtic language, which long prevailed in Britain.

[258] A deity of Scythian origin, called Frea or Fricca. See Mallet's Introduct. to Hist. of Denmark.

[259] Many vestiges of this superstition remain to this day in Sweden. The peasants, in the month of February, the season formerly sacred to Frea, make little images of boars in paste, which they apply to various superstitious uses. (See Eccard.) A figure of a Mater Deum, with the boar, is given by Mr. Pennant, in his Tour in Scotland, 1769, p. 268, engraven from a stone found at the great station at Netherby in Cumberland.

[260] The cause of this was, probably, their confined situation, which did not permit them to wander in hunting and plundering parties, like the rest of the Germans.

[261] This name was transferred to *glass* when it came into use. Pliny speaks of the production of amber in this country as follows:—"It is certain that amber is produced in the islands of the Northern Ocean, and is called by the Germans *gless*. One of these islands, by the natives named Austravia, was on this account called Glessaria by our sailors in the fleet of Germanicus."—Lib. xxxvii. 3.

[262] Much of the Prussian amber is even at present collected on the shores of the Baltic. Much also is found washed out of the clayey cliffs of Holderness. See Tour in Scotland, 1769, p. 16.

[263] Insomuch that the Guttones, who formerly inhabited this coast, made use of amber as fuel, and sold it for that purpose to the neighboring Teutones. (Plin. xxxvii. 2.)

[264] Various toys and utensils of amber, such as bracelets, necklaces, rings, cups, and even pillars, were to be met with among the luxurious Romans.

[265] In a work by Goeppert and Berendt, on "Amber and the Fossil Remains of Plants contained in it," published at Berlin, 1845, a passage is found (of which a translation is here given) which quite harmonizes with the account of Tacitus:—- "About the parts which are known by the name of Samland an island emerged, or rather a group of islands, ... which gradually increased in circumference, and, favored by a mild sea climate, was overspread with vegetation and forest. This forest was the means of amber being produced. Certain trees in it exuded gums in such quantities that the sunken forest soil now appears to be filled with it to such a degree, as if it had only been deprived of a very trifling part of its contents by the later eruptions of the sea, and the countless storms which have lashed the ocean for centuries." Hence, though found underground, it appears to have been originally the production of some resinous tree. Hence, too, the reason of the appearance of insects, &c. in it, as mentioned by Tacitus.

[266] Norwegians.

[267] All beyond the Vistula was reckoned Sarmatia. These people, therefore, were properly inhabitants of Sarmatia, though from their manners they appeared of German origin.

[268] Pliny also reckons the Peucini among the German nations:—"The fifth part of Germany is possessed by the Peucini and Bastarnae, who border on the Dacians." (iv. 14.) From Strabo it appears that the Peucini, part of the Bastarnae, inhabited the country about the mouths of the Danube, and particularly the island Peuce, now Piczina, formed by the river.

[269] The habitations of the Peucini were fixed; whereas the Sarmatians wandered about in their wagons.

[270] "Sordes omnium ac torpor; procerum connubiis mixtis nonnihil in Sarmatarum habitum foedantur." In many editions the semicolon is placed not after *torpor*, but after *procerum*. The sense of the passage so read is: "The chief men are lazy and stupid, besides being filthy, like all the rest. Intermarriage with the Sarmatians have debased." &c.

[271] The Venedi extended beyond the Peucini and Bastarnae as far as the Baltic Sea; where is the Sinus Venedicus, now the Gulf of Dantzig. Their name is also preserved in Wenden, a part of Livonia. When the German nations made their irruption into Italy, France and Spain, the Venedi, also called Winedi, occupied their

80

vacant settlements between the Vistula and Elbe. Afterwards they crossed the Danube, and seized Dalmatia, Illyricum, Istria, Carniola, and the Noric Alps. A part of Carniola still retains the name of Windismarck, derived from them. This people were also called Slavi; and their language, the Sclavonian, still prevails through a vast tract of country.

[272] This is still the manner of living of the successors of the Sarmatians, the Nogai Tartars.

[273] Their country is called by Pliny, Eningia, now Finland. Warnefrid (De Gest. Langobard. i. 5) thus describes their savage and wretched state:—"The Scritobini, or Scritofinni, are not without snow in the midst of summer; and, being little superior in sagacity to the brutes, live upon no other food than the raw flesh of wild animals, the hairy skins of which they use for clothing. They derive their name, according to the barbarian tongue, from leaping, because they hunt wild beasts by a certain method of leaping or springing with pieces of wood bent in the shape of a bow." Here is an evident description of the snow-shoes or raquets in common use among the North American savages, as well as the inhabitants of the most northern parts of Europe.

[274] As it is just after mentioned that their chief dependence is on the game procured in hunting, this can only mean that the vegetable food they use consists of wild herbs, in opposition to the cultivated products of the earth.

[275] The Esquimaux and the South Sea islanders do the same thing to this day.

[276] People of Lapland. The origin of this fable was probably the manner of clothing in these cold regions, where the inhabitants bury themselves in the thickest furs, scarcely leaving anything of the form of a human creature.

[277] It is with true judgment that this excellent historian forbears to intermix fabulous narrations with the very interesting and instructive matter of this treatise. Such a mixture might have brought an impeachment on the fidelity of the account in general; which, notwithstanding the suspicions professed by some critics, contains nothing but what is entirely consonant to truth and nature. Had Tacitus indulged his invention in the description of German manners, is it probable that he could have given so just a picture of the state of a people under similar circumstances, the savage tribes of North America, as we have seen them within the present century? Is it likely that his relations would have been so admirably confirmed by the codes of law still extant of the several German nations; such as the Salic, Ripuary, Burgundian, English and Lombard? or that after the course of so many centuries, and the numerous changes of empire, the customs, laws and manners he describes should still be traced in all the various people of German derivation? As long as the original constitution and jurisprudence of our own and other European countries are studied, this treatise will be regarded as one of the most precious and authentic monuments of historical antiquity.

THE LIFE OF CNAEUS JULIUS AGRICOLA.

[1] Rutilius was consul B.C. 104; and for his upright life and great strictness was banished B.C. 92. Tacitus is the only writer who says he wrote his own life. Athenaeus mentions that he wrote a history of the affairs of Rome in the Greek language. Scaurus was consul B.C. 114, and again B.C. 106. He is the same Scaurus whom Sallust mentions as having been bribed by Jugurtha. As the banishment of Rutilius took place on the accusation of Scaurus, it is possible that, when the former wrote his life, the latter also wrote his, in order to defend himself from charges advanced against him.

[2] *Venia opus fuit.* This whole passage has greatly perplexed the critics. The text is disputed, and it is not agreed why Tacitus asks indulgence. Brotier, Dronke, and others, say he asks indulgence for the inferiority of his style and manner *(incondita ac rudi voce,* c. 3), as compared with the distinguished authors *(quisque celeberrimus)* of an earlier and better age. But there would have been no less occasion to apologize for that, if the times he wrote of had not been so hostile to virtue. Hertel, La Bletterie, and many French critics, understand that he apologizes for writing the memoir of his father-in-law so late *(nunc),* when he was already dead *(defuncti),* instead of doing it, as the great men of a former day did, while the subject of their memoirs was yet alive; and he pleads, in justification of the delay, that he could not have written it earlier without encountering the dangers of that cruel age (the age of Domitian). This makes a very good sense. The only objection against it is, that the language, *opus fuit,* seems rather to imply that it was necessary to justify himself for writing it at all, by citing the examples of former distinguished writers of biography, as he had done in the foregoing introduction. But why would it have been unnecessary to apologize for writing the life of Agricola, if the times in which he lived had not been so unfriendly to virtue? Because then Agricola would have had opportunity to achieve victories and honors, which would have demanded narration, but for which the jealousy and cruelty of Domitian now gave no scope. This is the explanation of Roth; and he supports it by reference to the fact, that the achievements of Agricola in the conquest of Britain, though doubtless just as Tacitus has described them, yet occupy so small a space in general history, that they are not even mentioned by any ancient historian except Dio Cassius; and he mentions them chiefly out of regard to the discovery made by Agricola, for the first time, that Britain was an island (Vid. R. Exc. 1.) This explanation answers all the demands of grammar and logic; but as a matter of taste and feeling, I cannot receive it. Such an apology for the unworthiness of his subject at the commencement of the biography, ill accords with the tone of dignified confidence which pervades the memoir. The best commentary I have seen on the passage is that of Walther; and it would not, perhaps, be giving more space to so mooted a question than the scholar requires, to extract it entire:—"*Venia,*" he says, "is here nothing else than what we, in the language of modesty, call an apology, and has respect to the very justification he has just offered in the foregoing exordium. For Tacitus there appeals to the usage, not of remote antiquity only, but of later times also, to justify his design of writing the biography of a distinguished man. There would have been no need of such an apology in other times. In other times, dispensing with all preamble, he would have

begun, as in c. 4, 'Cnaeus Julius Agricola,' &c., assured that no one would question the propriety of his course. But now, after a long and servile silence, when one begins again 'facta moresque posteris tradere,' when he utters the first word where speech and almost memory (c. 2) had so long been lost, when he stands forth as the first vindicator of condemned virtue, he seems to venture on something so new, so strange, so bold, that it may well require apology." In commenting upon *cursaturus—tempora*, Walther adds: "If there is any boldness in the author's use of words here, that very fact suits the connection, that by the complexion of his language even, he might paint the audacity 'cursandi tam saeva et infesta virtutibus tempora'—of running over (as in a race, for such is Walther's interpretation of *cursandi*) times so cruel and so hostile to virtue. Not that those times could excite in Tacitus any real personal fear, for they were past, and he could now think what he pleased, and speak what he thought (Hist. i. 1). Still he shudders at the recollection of those cruelties; and he treads with trembling footstep, as it were, even the path lately obstructed by them. He looks about him to see whether, even now, he may safely utter his voice, and he timidly asks pardon for venturing to break the reigning silence."—*Tyler.*

[3] A passage in Dio excellently illustrates the fact here referred to: "He (Domitian) put to death Rusticus Arulenus, because he studied philosophy, and had given Thrasea the appellation of holy; and Herennius Senecio, because, although he lived many years after serving the office of quaestor, he solicited no other post, and because he had written the Life of Helvidius Priscus." (lxvii. p. 765.) With less accuracy, Suetonius, in his Life of Domitian (s. 10), says: "He put to death Junius Rusticus, because he had published the panegyrics of Paetus Thrasea and Helvidius Priscus, and had styled them most holy persons; and on this occasion he expelled all the philosophers from the city, and from. Italy." Arulenus Rusticus was a Stoic; on which account he was contumeliously called by M. Regulus "the ape of the Stoics, marked with the Vitellian scar." (Pliny, Epist. i. 5.) Thrasea, who killed Nero, is particularly recorded in the Annals, book xvi.

[4] The expulsion of the philosophers, mentioned in the passage above quoted from Suetonius.

[5] This truly happy period began when, after the death of Domitian, and the recision of his acts, the imperial authority devolved on Nerva, whose virtues were emulated by the successive emperors, Trajan, Hadrian, and both the Antonines.

[6] *Securitas publica*, "the public security," was a current expression and wish, and was frequently inscribed on medals.

[7] The term of Domitian's reign.

[8] It appears that at this time Tacitus proposed to write not only the books of his History and Annals, which contain the "memorial of past servitude," but an account of the "present blessings" exemplified in the occurrences under Nerva and Trajan.

[9] There were two Roman colonies of this name; one in Umbria, supposed to be the place now called Friuli; the other in Narbonnensian Gaul, the modern name of which is Frejus. This last was probably the birth-place of Agricola.

[10] Of the procurators who were sent to the provinces, some had the charge of the public revenue; others, not only of that, but of the private revenue of the emperor. These were the imperial procurators. All the offices relative to the finances were in the possession of the Roman knights; of whom the imperial procurators were accounted noble. Hence the equestrian nobility of which Tacitus speaks. In some of the lesser provinces, the procurators had the civil jurisdiction, as well at the administration of the revenue. This was the case in Judaea.

[11] Seneca bears a very honorable testimony to this person, "If," says he, "we have occasion for an example of a great mind, let us cite that of Julius Graecinus, an excellent person, whom Caius Cæsar put to death on this account alone, that he was a better man than could be suffered under a tyrant." (De Benef. ii. 21.) His books concerning Vineyards are commended by Columella and Pliny.

[12] Caligula.

[13] Marcus Silanus was the father of Claudia, the first wife of Caius. According to the historians of that period, Caius was jealous of him, and took every opportunity of mortifying him. Tacitus (Hist. iv. 48) mentions that the emperor deprived him of the military command of the troops in Africa in an insulting manner. Dion (lix.) states, that when, from his age and rank, Silanus was usually asked his opinion first in the senate, the worth. Suetonius (iv. 23) records that the emperor one day put to sea in a hasty manner, and commanded Silanus to follow him. This, from fear of illness, he declined to do; upon which the emperor, alleging that he stayed on shore in order to get possession of the city in case any accident befell himself, compelled him to cut his own throat. It would seem, from the present passage of Tacitus, that there were some legal forms taken in the case of Silanus, and that Julius Graecinus was ordered to be the accuser; and that that noble-minded man, refusing to take part in proceedings so cruel and iniquitous, was himself put to death.

[14] Of the part the Roman matrons took in the education of youth, Tacitus has given an elegant and interesting account, in his Dialogue concerning Oratory, c. 28.

[15] Now Marseilles. This was a colony of the Phocaeans; whence it derived that Grecian politeness for which it was long famous.

[16] It was usual for generals to admit young men of promising characters to this honorable companionship, which resembled the office of an aide-de-camp in the modern service. Thus, Suetonius informs us that Cæsar made his first campaign in Asia as tent-companion to Marcus Thermus the praetor.

[17] This was the fate of the colony of veterans at Camalodunum, now Colchester or Maldon. A particular account of this revolt is given in the 14th book of the Annals.

[18] This alludes to the defeat of Petilius Cerialis, who came with the ninth legion to succor the colony of Camalodunum. All the infantry were slaughtered; and Petilius, with the cavalry alone, got away to the camp. It was shortly after this, that Suetonius defeated Boadicea and her forces.

[19] Those of Nero.

[20] The office of quaestor was the entrance to all public employments. The quaestors and their secretaries were distributed by lot to the several provinces, that there might be no previous connections between them and the governors, but they might serve as checks upon each other.

[21] Brother of the emperor Otho.

[22] At the head of the praetors, the number of whom was different at different periods of the empire, were the Praetor Urbanus, and Praetor Peregrinus. The first administered justice among the citizens, the second among strangers. The rest presided at public debates, and had the charge of exhibiting the public games, which were celebrated with great solemnity for seven successive days, and at a vast expense. This, indeed, in the times of the emperors, was almost the sole business of the praetors, whose dignity, as Tacitus expresses it, consisted in the idle trappings of state; whence Boethius justly terms the praetorship "an empty name, and a grievous burthen on the senatorian rank."

[23] Nero had plundered the temples for the supply of his extravagance and debauchery. See Annals, xv. 45.

[24] This was the year of Rome 822; from the birth of Christ, 69.

[25] The cruelties and depredations committed on the coast of Italy by this fleet are described in lively colors by Tacitus, Hist. ii. 12, 13.

[26] Now the county of Vintimiglia. The attack upon the municipal town of this place, called Albium Intemelium, is particularly mentioned in the passage above referred to.

[27] In the month of July of this year.

[28] The twentieth legion, surnamed the Victorious, was stationed in Britain at Deva, the modern Chester, where many inscriptions and other monuments of Roman antiquities have been discovered.

[29] Roscius Caelius. His disputes with the governor of Britain, Trebellius Maximus, are related by Tacitus, Hist. i. 60.

[30] The governors of the province, and commanders in chief over all the legions stationed in it.

[31] He had formerly been commander of the ninth legion.

[32] The province of Aquitania extended from the Pyrenean mountains to the river Liger (Loire).

[33] The governors of the neighboring provinces.

[34] Agricola was consul in the year of Rome 830, A.D. 77, along with Domitian. They succeeded, in the calends of July, the consuls Vespasian and Titus, who began the year.

[35] He was admitted into the Pontifical College, at the head of which was the Pontifex Maximus.

[36] Julius Cæsar, Livy, Strabo, Fabius Rusticus, Pomponius Mela, Pliny, &c.

[37] Thus Cæsar: "One side of Britain inclines towards Spain, and the setting sun; on which part Ireland is situated."—Bell. Gall. v. 13.

[38] These, as well as other resemblances suggested by ancient geographers, have been mostly destroyed by the greater accuracy of modern maps.

[39] This is so far true, that the northern extremity of Scotland is much narrower than the southern coast of England.

[40] The Orkney Islands. These, although now first thoroughly known to the Romans, had before been heard of, and mentioned by authors. Thus Mela, in. 6: "There are thirty of the Orcades, separated from each other by narrow straits." And Pliny, iv. 16: "The Orcades are forty in number, at a small distance from each other." In the reign of Claudius, the report concerning these islands was particularly current, and adulation converted it into the news of a victory. Hence Hieronymus in his Chronicon says, "Claudius triumphed over the Britons, and added the Orcades to the Roman empire."

[41] Camden supposes the Shetland Islands to be meant here by Thule; others imagine it to have been one of the Hebrides. Pliny, iv. 16, mentions Thule as the most remote of all known islands; and, by placing it but one day's sail from the Frozen Ocean, renders it probable that Iceland was intended. Procopius (Bell. Goth, ii. 15) speaks of another Thule, which must have been Norway, which many of the

86

ancients thought to be an island. Mr. Pennant supposes that the Thule here meant was Foula, a very lofty isle, one of the most westerly of the Shetlands, which might easily be descried by the fleet.

[42] As far as the meaning of this passage can be elucidated, it would appear as if the first circumnavigators of Britain, to enhance the idea of their dangers and hardships, had represented the Northern sea as in such a thickened half solid state, that the oars could scarcely be worked, or the water agitated by winds. Tacitus, however, rather chooses to explain its stagnant condition from the want of winds, and the difficulty of moving so great a body of waters. But the fact, taken either way, is erroneous; as this sea is never observed frozen, and is remarkably stormy and tempestuous.—-*Aiken.*

[43] The great number of firths and inlets of the sea, which almost cut through the northern parts of the island, as well as the height of the tides on the coast, render this observation peculiarly proper.

[44] Cæsar mentions that the interior inhabitants of Britain were supposed to have originated in the island itself. (Bell. Gall. v. 12.)

[45] Caledonia, now Scotland, was at that time overspread by vast forests. Thus Pliny, iv. 16, speaking of Britain, says, that "for thirty years past the Roman arms had not extended the knowledge of the island beyond the Caledonian forest."

[46] Inhabitants of what are now the counties of Glamorgan, Monmouth, Brecknock, Hereford, and Radnor.

[47] The Iberi were a people of Spain, so called from their neighborhood to the river Iberus, now Ebro.

[48] Of these, the inhabitants of Kent are honorably mentioned by Cæsar. "Of all these people, by far the most civilized are those inhabiting the maritime country of Cantium, who differ little in their manners from the Gauls."—Bell. Gall. v. 14.

[48] From the obliquity of the opposite coasts of England and France, some part of the former runs further south than the northern extremity of the latter.

[50] Particularly the mysterious and bloody solemnities of the Druids.

[51] The children were born and nursed in this ferocity. Thus Solinus, c. 22, speaking of the warlike nation of Britons, says, "When a woman is delivered of a male child, she lays its first food upon the husband's sword, and with the point gently puts it within the little one's mouth, praying to her country deities that his death may in like manner be in the midst of arms."

[52] In the reign of Claudius.

[53] The practice of the Greeks in the Homeric age was the reverse of this.

[54] Thus the kings Cunobelinus, Caractacus, and Prasutagus, and the queens Cartismandua and Boadicea, are mentioned in different parts of Tacitus.

[55] Cæsar says of Britain, "the climate is more temperate than that of Gaul, the cold being less severe." (Bell. Gall. v. 12.) This certainly proceeds from its insular situation, and the moistness of its atmosphere.

[56] Thus Pliny (ii. 75):—"The longest day in Italy is of fifteen hours, in Britain of seventeen, where in summer the nights are light."

[57] Tacitus, through the medium of Agricola, must have got this report, either from the men of Scandinavia, or from those of the Britons who had passed into that country, or been informed to this effect by those who had visited it. It is quite true, that in the further part of Norway, and so also again in Iceland and the regions about the North Pole, there is, at the summer solstice, an almost uninterrupted day for nearly two months. Tacitus here seems to affirm this as universally the case, not having heard that, at the winter solstice, there is a night of equal duration.

[58] Tacitus, after having given the report of the Britons as he had heard it, probably from Agricola, now goes on to state his own views on the subject. He represents that, as the far north is level, there is nothing, when the sun is in the distant horizon, to throw up a shadow towards the sky: that the light, indeed, is intercepted from the surface of the earth itself, and so there is darkness upon it; but that the sky above is still clear and bright from its rays. And hence he supposes that the brightness of the upper regions neutralizes the darkness on the earth, forming a degree of light equivalent to the evening twilight or the morning dawn, or, indeed, rendering it next to impossible to decide when the evening closes and the morning begins. Compare the following account, taken from a "Description of a Visit to Shetland," in vol. viii. of Chambers' Miscellany:—"Being now in the 60th degree of north latitude, daylight could scarcely be said to have left us during the night, and at 2 o'clock in the morning, albeit the mist still hung about us, we could see as clearly as we can do in London, at about any hour in a November day."

[59] Mr. Pennant has a pleasing remark concerning the soil and climate of our island, well agreeing with that of Tacitus:—"The climate of Great Britain is above all others productive of the greatest variety and abundance of wholesome vegetables, which, to crown our happiness, are almost equally diffused through all its parts: this general fertility is owing to those clouded skies, which foreigners mistakenly urge as a reproach on our country: but let us cheerfully endure a temporary gloom, which clothes not only our meadows, but our hills, with the richest verdure."—Brit. Zool. 4to. i. 15.

[60] Strabo (iv. 138) testifies the same. Cicero, on the other hand, asserts, that not a single grain of silver is found on this island. (Ep. ad Attic, iv. 16.) If we have recourse to modern authorities, we find Camden mentioning gold and silver mines in

Cumberland, silver in Flintshire, and gold in Scotland. Dr. Borlase (Hist. of Cornwall, p. 214) relates, that so late as the year 1753, several pieces of gold were found in what the miners call stream tin; and silver is now got in considerable quantity from several of our lead ores. A curious paper, concerning the Gold Mines of Scotland, is given by Mr. Pennant in Append. (No. x.) to his second part of a "Tour in Scotland in 1772," and a much more general account of the mines and ores of Great Britain in early times, in his "Tour in Wales of 1773," pp. 51-66.

[61] Camden mentions pearls being found in the counties of Caernarvon and Cumberland, and in the British sea. Mr. Pennant, in his "Tour in Scotland in 1769," takes notice of a considerable pearl fishery out of the fresh-water mussel, in the vicinity of Perth, from whence 10,000_l._ worth of pearls were sent to London from 1761 to 1764. It was, however, almost exhausted when he visited the country. See also the fourth volume of Mr. Pennant's Br. Zool. (Class vi. No. 18), where he gives a much more ample account of the British pearls. Origen, in his Comment. on Matthew, pp. 210, 211, gives a description of the British pearl, which, he says, was next in value to the Indian;—"Its surface is of a gold color, but it is cloudy, and less transparent than the Indian." Pliny speaks of the British unions as follows:—"It is certain that small and discolored ones are produced in Britain; since the deified Julius has given us to understand that the breastplate which he dedicated to Venus Genitrix, and placed in her temple, was made of British pearls."—ix. 35.

[62] Caesar's two expeditions into Britain were in the years of Rome 699 and 700. He himself gives an account of them, and they are also mentioned by Strabo and Dio.

[63] It was the wise policy of Augustus not to extend any further the limits of the empire; and with regard to Britain, in particular, he thought the conquest and preservation of it would be attended with more expense than it could repay. (Strabo, ii. 79, and iv. 138.) Tiberius, who always professed an entire deference for the maxims and injunctions of Augustus, in this instance, probably, was convinced of their propriety.

[64] Caligula.

[65] Claudius invaded Britain in the year of Rome 796, A.D. 43.

[66] In the parish of Dinder, near Hereford, are yet remaining the vestiges of a Roman encampment, called Oyster-hill, as is supposed from this Ostorius. Camden's Britain, by Gibson, p. 580.

[67] That of Camalodunum, now Colchester, or Maldon.

[68] The Mona of Tacitus is the Isle of Anglesey, that of Cæsar is the Isle of Man, called by Pliny Monapia.

[69] The avarice of Catus Decidianus the procurator is mentioned as the cause by which the Britons were forced into this war, by Tacitus, Annal. xiv. 32.

[70] Julius Classicianus, who succeeded Decidianus, was at variance with the governor, but was no less oppressive to the province.

[71] By the slaughter of Varus.

[72] The Rhine and Danube.

[73] Boadicea, whose name is variously written Boudicea, Bonduca, Voadicea, &c., was queen of the Iceni, or people of Suffolk, Norfolk, Cambridgeshire, and Huntingdonshire. A particular account of this revolt is given in the Annals, xiv. 31, and seq.

[74] Of Camalodunum.

[75] This was in A.D. 61. According to Tac. Hist. i. 6, Petronius Turpilianus was put to death by Galba, A.D. 68.

[76] The date of his arrival is uncertain.

[77] He was sent to Britain by Vespasian, A.D. 69.

[78] The Brigantes inhabited Yorkshire, Lancashire, Westmoreland, Cumberland, and Durham.

[79] The date of his arrival in Britain is uncertain. This Frontinus is the author of the work on "Stratagems," and, at the time of his appointment to the lieutenancy of Britain, he was *curator aquarum* at Rome. This, probably, it was that induced him to write his other work on the aqueducts of Rome.

[80] This seems to relate to his having been curtailed in his military operations by the parsimony of Vespasian, who refused him permission to attack other people than the Silures. See c. 11.

[81] Where these people inhabited is mentioned in p. 355, note 5.

[82] This was in the year of Rome 831, of Christ 78.

[83] Inhabitants of North Wales, exclusive of the Isle of Anglesey.

[84] *I.e.* Some were for immediate action, others for delay. Instead of *et quibus*, we read with Dr. Smith's edition (London, 1850), *ut quibus*.

[85] *Vexilla* is here used for *vexillarii*. "Under the Empire the name of Vexillarii was given to a distinct body of soldiers supposed to have been composed of veterans, who were released from the military oath and regular service, but kept embodied under a separate flag (*vexillum*), to render assistance to the army if required, guard the frontier, and garrison recently conquered provinces; a certain number of these supernumeraries being attached to each legion. (Tac. Hist. ii. 83, 100; Ann. i. 36.)"—Rich, Comp. to Dict. and Lex. s. v. Vexillum.

[86] A pass into the vale of Clwyd, in the parish of Llanarmon, is still called Bwlch Agrikle, probably from having been occupied by Agricola, in his road to Mona.—— *Mr. Pennant.*

[87] From this circumstance it would appear that these auxiliaries were Batavians, whose skill in this practice is related by Tacitus, Hist. iv. 12.

[88] It was customary for the Roman generals to decorate with sprigs of laurel the letters in which they sent home the news of any remarkable success. Thus Pliny, xv. 30: "The laurel, the principal messenger of joy and victory among the Romans, is affixed to letters, and to the spears and javelins of the soldiers." The *laurus* of the ancients was probably the baytree, and not what we now call laurel.

[89] *Ascire*, al. *accire*, "To receive into regular service." The reference is to the transfer of soldiers from the supernumeraries to the legions. So Walch, followed by Dronke, Both, and Walther. The next clause implies, that he took care to receive into the service none but the best men (*optimum quemque*), who, he was confident, would prove faithful (*fidelissimum*).

[90] In like manner Suetonius says of Julius Cæsar, "He neither noticed nor punished every crime; but while he strictly inquired into and rigorously punished desertion and mutiny, he connived at other delinquencies."—Life of Julius Cæsar, s. 67.

[91] Many commentators propose reading "exaction," instead of "augmentation." But the latter may be suffered to remain, especially as Suetonius informs us that "Vespasian, not contented with renewing some taxes remitted under Galba, added new and heavy ones: and augmented the tributes paid by the provinces, even doubling some."—Life of Vesp. s. 19.

[92] In the year of Rome 832. A.D. 79.

[93] Many vestiges of these or other Roman camps yet remain in different parts of Great Britain. Two principal ones, in the county of Annandale, in Scotland, called Burnswork and Middleby, are described at large by Gordon in his Itiner. Septentrion, pp. 16, 18.

[94] The year of Rome 833, A.D. 80.

[95] Now the Firth of Tay.

[96] The principal of these was at Ardoch, seated so as to command the entrance into two valleys, Strathallan and Strathearn. A description and plan of its remains, still in good preservation, are given by Mr. Pennant in his Tour in Scotland in 1772, part ii. p. 101.

[97] The year of Rome 834, A.D. 81.

[98] The Firths of Clyde and Forth.

[99] The neck of land between these opposite arms of the sea is only about thirty miles over. About fifty-five years after Agricola had left the island, Lollius Urbicus, governor of Britain under Antoninus Pius, erected a vast wall or rampart, extending from Old Kirkpatrick on the Clyde, to Caeridden, two miles west of Abercorn, on the Forth, a space of nearly thirty-seven miles, defended by twelve or thirteen forts. These are supposed to have been on the site of those of Agricola. This wall is usually called Graham's dike; and some parts of it are now subsisting.

[100] The year of Rome 835, A.D. 82.

[101] Crossing the Firth of Clyde, or Dumbarton Bay, and turning to the western coast of Argyleshire, or the Isles of Arran and Bute.

[102] The Bay of Biscay.

[103] The Mediterranean.

[104] The year of Rome 836, A.D. 83.

[105] The eastern parts of Scotland, north of the Firth of Forth, where now are the counties of Fife, Kinross, Perth, Angus, &c.

[106] This legion, which had been weakened by many engagements, was afterwards recruited, and then called Gemina. Its station at this affair is supposed by Gordon to have been Lochore in Fifeshire. Mr. Pennant rather imagines the place of the attack to have been Comerie in Perthshire.

[107] For an account of these people see Manners of the Germans, c. 32.

[108] Mr. Pennant had a present made him in Skye, of a brass sword and a denarius found in that island. Might they not have been lost by some of these people in one of their landings?

[109] The Rhine.

[110] This extraordinary expedition, according to Dio, set out from the western side of the island. They therefore must have coasted all that part of Scotland, must have passed the intricate navigation through the Hebrides, and the dangerous strait of Pentland Firth, and, after coming round to the eastern side, must have been driven to the mouth of the Baltic Sea, Here they lost their ships; and, in their attempt to proceed homeward by land, were seized as pirates, part by the Suevi, and the rest by the Frisii.

[111] The year of Rome 837, A.D. 84.

[112] The scene of this celebrated engagement is by Gordon (Itin. Septent.) supposed to be in Strathern, near a place now called the Kirk of Comerie, where are the remains of two Roman camps. Mr. Pennant, however, in his Tour in 1772, part ii. p. 96, gives reasons which appear well founded for dissenting from Gordon's opinion.

[113] The more usual spelling of this name is Galgacus; but the other is preferred as of better authority.

[114] "Peace given to the world" is a very frequent inscription on the Roman medals.

[115] It was the Roman policy to send the recruits raised in the provinces to some distant country, for fear of their desertion or revolt.

[116] How much this was the fate of the Romans themselves, when, in the decline of the empire, they were obliged to pay tribute to the surrounding barbarians, is shown in lively colors by Salvian:—"We call that a gift which is a purchase, and a purchase of a condition the most hard and miserable. For all captives, when they are once redeemed, enjoy their liberty: we are continually paying a ransom, yet are never free."—De Gubern. Dei, vi.

[118] The expedition of Claudius into Britain was in the year of Rome 796, from which to the period of this engagement only forty-two years were elapsed. The number fifty therefore is given oratorically rather than accurately.

[119] The Latin word used here, *covinarius*, signifies the driver of a *covinus*, or chariot, the axle of which was bent into the form of a scythe. The British manner of fighting from chariots is particularly described by Cæsar, who gives them the name of *esseda*:—"The following is the manner of fighting from *essedae*: They first drive round with them to all parts of the line, throwing their javelins, and generally disordering the ranks by the very alarm occasioned by the horses, and the rattling of the wheels: then, as soon as they have insinuated themselves between the troops of horse, they leap from their chariots and fight on foot. The drivers then withdraw a little from the battle, in order that, if their friends are overpowered by numbers, they may have a secure retreat to the chariots. Thus they act with the celerity of horse, and the stability of foot; and by daily use and exercise they acquire the power of

holding up their horses at full speed down a steep declivity, of stopping them suddenly, and turning in a short compass; and they accustom themselves to run upon the pole, and stand on the cross-tree, and from thence with great agility to recover their place in the chariot."—Bell. Gall. iv. 33.

[120] These targets, called *cetrae*, in the Latin, were made of leather. The broad sword and target were till very lately the peculiar arms of the Highlanders.

[121] Several inscriptions have been found in Britain commemorating the Tungrian cohorts.

[122] The great conciseness of Tacitus has rendered the description of this battle somewhat obscure. The following, however, seems to have been the general course of occurrences in it:—The foot on both sides began the engagement. The first line of the Britons which was formed on the plain being broken, the Roman auxiliaries advanced up the hill after them. In the meantime the Roman horse in the wings, unable to withstand the shock of the chariots, gave way, and were pursued by the British chariots and horse, which then fell in among the Roman infantry, These, who at first had relaxed their files to prevent their being out-fronted, now closed, in order better to resist the enemy, who by this means were unable to penetrate them. The chariots and horse, therefore, became entangled amidst the inequalities of the ground, and the thick ranks of the Romans; and, no longer able to wheel and career as upon the open plain, gave not the least appearance of an equestrian skirmish: but, keeping their footing with difficulty on the declivity, were pushed off, and scattered in disorder over the field.

[123] People of Fifeshire.

[124] Where this was does not appear. Brotier calls it Sandwich, making it the same as *Rutupium*: others Plymouth or Portsmouth. It is clear, however, this cannot be the case, from the subsequent words.—*White.*

[125] This circumnavigation was in a contrary direction to that of the Usipian deserters, the fleet setting out from the Firth of Tay on the eastern coast, and sailing round the northern, western, and southern coasts, till it arrived at the port of Sandwich in Kent. After staying here some time to refit, it went to its former station, in the Firth of Forth, or Tay.

[126] It was in this same year that Domitian made his pompous expedition into Germany, from whence he returned without ever seeing the enemy.

[127] Caligula in like manner got a number of tall men with their hair dyed red to give credit to a pretended victory over the Germans.

[128] Thus Pliny, in his Panegyric on Trajan, xlviii., represents Domitian as "ever affecting darkness and secrecy, and never emerging from his solitude but in order to make a solitude."

[129] Not the triumph itself, which, after the year of Rome 740 was no longer granted to private persons, but reserved for the imperial family. This new piece of adulation was invented by Agrippa in order to gratify Augustus. The "triumphal ornaments" which were still bestowed, were a peculiar garment, statue, and other insignia which had distinguished the person of the triumphing general.

[130] Of Dover.

[131] Domitian, it seems, was afraid that Agricola might refuse to obey the recall he forwarded to him, and even maintain his post by force. He therefore despatched one of his confidential freedmen with an autograph letter, wherein he was informed Syria was given to him as his province. This, however, was a mere ruse: and hence it was not to be delivered as Agricola had already set out on his return. In compliance with these instructions, the freedman returned at once to Domitian, when he found Agricola on his passage to Rome According to Dion (liii.), the emperor's lieutenants were required to leave their province immediately upon the arrival of their successor, and return to Rome within three months.— *White*.

[132] Agricola's successor in Britain appears to have been Sallustius Lucullus, who, as Suetonius informs us, was put to death by Domitian because he, permitted certain lances of a new construction to be palled Lucullean.—Life of Domitian, s. 10.

[133] Of this worst kind of enemies, who praise a man in order to render him obnoxious, the emperor Julian, who had himself suffered greatly by them, speaks feelingly in his 12th epistle to Basilius;—"For we live together not in that state of dissimulation, which, I imagine, you have hitherto experienced: in which those who praise you, hate you with a more confirmed aversion than your most inveterate enemies,"

[134] These calamitous events are recorded by Suetonius in his Life of Domitian.

[135] The Rhine and Danube.

[136] The two senior consulars cast lots for the government of Asia and Africa.

[137] Suetonius relates that Civica Cerealis was put to death in his proconsulate of Asia, on the charge of meditating a revolt. (Life of Domitian, s. 10.)

[138] Obliging persons to return thanks for an injury was a refinement in tyranny frequently practised by the worst of the Roman emperors. Thus Seneca informs us, that "Caligula was thanked by those whose children had been put to death, and whose property had been confiscated." (De Tranquil, xiv.) And again;—"The reply

of a person who had grown old in his attendance on kings, when he was asked how he had attained a thing so uncommon in courts as old age? is well known. It was, said he, by receiving injuries, and returning thanks."—De Ira, ii. 33.

[139] From a passage in Dio, lxxviii. p. 899, this sum appears to have been *decies sestertium*, about 9,000_l._ sterling.

[140] Thus Seneca: "Little souls rendered insolent by prosperity have this worst property, that they hate those whom they have injured."—De Ira, ii. 33.

[141] Several who suffered under Nero and Domitian erred, though nobly, in this respect.

[142] A Greek epigram still extant of Antiphilus, a Byzantine, to the memory of a certain Agricola, is supposed by the learned to refer to the great man who is the subject of this work. It is in the Anthologia, lib. i. tit. 37.

[143] Dio absolutely affirms it; but from the manner in which Tacitus, who had better means of information, speaks of it, the story was probably false.

[144] It appears that the custom of making the emperor co-heir with the children of the testator was not by any means uncommon. It was done in order to secure the remainder to the family. Thus Prasutagus, king of the Iceni in Britain, made Nero co-heir with his two daughters. Thus when Lucius Vetus was put to death by Nero, his friends urged him to leave part of his property to the emperor, that his grandsons might enjoy the rest. (Ann. xvi. 11.) Suetonius (viii. 17) mentions that Domitian used to seize the estates of persons the most unknown to him, if any one could be found to assert that the deceased had expressed an intention to make the emperor his heir.—*White.*

[145] Caligula. This was A.D. 40, when he was sole consul.

[146] According to this account, the birth of Agricola was on June 13th, in the year of Rome 793, A.D. 40; and his death on August 23d, in the year of Rome 846 A.D. 93: for this appears by the Fasti Consulares to have been the year of the consulate of Collega and Priscus. He was therefore only in his fifty-fourth year when he died; so that the copyists must probably have written by mistake LVI. instead of LIV.

[147] From this representation, Dio appears to have been mistaken in asserting that Agricola passed the latter part of his life in dishonor and penury.

[148] Juvenal breaks out in a noble strain of indignation against this savage cruelty, which distinguished the latter part of Domitian's reign:

Atque utinam his potius nugis tota illa dedisset
Tempora saevitiae: claras quibus abstulit Urbi

Illustresque animas impune, et vindice nullo.
Sed periit, postquam cerdonibus esse timendus
Coeperat: hoc nocuit Lamiarum, caede madenti.—Sat. iv. 150.

"What folly this! but oh! that all the rest
Of his dire reign had thus been spent in jest!
And all that time such trifles had employ'd
In which so many nobles he destroy'd!
He safe, they unrevenged, to the disgrace
Of the surviving, tame, patrician race!
But when he dreadful to the rabble grew,
  Him, who so many lords had slain, they slew."—DUKE.

[149] This happened in the year of Rome 848.

[150] Carus and Massa, who were proverbially infamous as informers, are represented by Juvenal as dreading a still more dangerous villain, Heliodorus.

—Quem Massa timet, quem munere palpat
Carus.—Sat. i. 35.

"Whom Massa dreads, whom Carus soothes with bribes."

Carus is also mentioned with deserved infamy by Pliny and Martial. He was a mimic by profession.

[151] Of this odious instrument of tyranny, Pliny the younger thus speaks: "The conversation turned upon Catullus Messalinus, whose loss of sight added the evils of blindness to a cruel disposition. He was irreverent, unblushing, unpitying, Like a weapon, of itself blind and unconscious, he was frequently hurled by Domitian against every man of worth." (iv. 22.) Juvenal launches the thunder of invective against him in the following lines:—

Et cum mortifero prudens Vejento Catullo,
Qui numquam visae flagrabat amore puellae,
Grande, et conspicuum nostro quoque tempore monstrum,
Caecus adulator, dirusque a ponte satelles,
Dignus Aricinos qui mendicaret ad axes,
Blandaque devexae jactaret basia rhedae.—Sat. iv. 113.

"Cunning Vejento next, and by his side
Bloody Catullus leaning on his guide:
Decrepit, yet a furious lover he,
And deeply smit with charms he could not see.
A monster, that ev'n this worst age outvies,
Conspicuous and above the common size.

A blind base flatterer; from some bridge or gate,
Raised to a murd'ring minister of state.
Deserving still to beg upon the road,
And bless each passing wagon and its load."—DUKE.

[152] This was a famous villa of Domitian's, near the site of the ancient Alba, about twelve miles from Rome. The place is now called Albano, and vast ruins of its magnificent edifices still remain.

[153] Tacitus, in his History, mentions this Massa Baebius as a person most destructive to all men of worth, and constantly engaged on the side of villains. From a letter of Pliny's to Tacitus, it appears that Herennius Senecio and himself were joined as counsel for the province of Boetica in a prosecution of Massa Baebius; and that Massa after his condemnation petitioned the consuls for liberty to prosecute Senecio for treason.

[154] By "our own hands," Tacitus means one of our own body, a senator. As Publicius Certus had seized upon Helvidius and led him to prison, Tacitus imputes the crime to the whole senatorian order. To the same purpose Pliny observes: "Amidst the numerous villanies of numerous persons, nothing appeared more atrocious than that in the senate-house one senator should lay hands on another, a praetorian on a consular man, a judge on a criminal."—B. ix. ep. 13.

[155] Helvidius Priscus, a friend of Pliny the younger, who did not suffer his death to remain unrevenged. See the Epistle above referred to.

[156] There is in this place some defect in the manuscripts, which critics have endeavored to supply in different manners. Brotier seems to prefer, though he does not adopt in the text, "nos Mauricum Rusticumque divisimus," "we parted Mauricus and Rusticus," by the death of one and the banishment of the other. The prosecution and crime of Rusticus (Arulenus) is mentioned at the beginning of this piece, c. 2. Mauricus was his brother.

[157] Herennius Senecio. See c. 2.

[158] Thus Pliny, in his Panegyr. on Trajan, xlviii.: "Domitian was terrible even to behold; pride in his brow, anger in his eyes, a feminine paleness in the rest of his body, in his face shamelessness suffused in a glowing red." Seneca, in Epist. xi. remarks, that "some are never more to be dreaded than when they blush; as if they had effused all their modesty. Sylla was always most furious when the blood had mounted into his cheeks."